Buying and Selling Pictures Successfully

Buying and Selling Pictures Successfully

ALAN G. THOMPSON

ROBERT HALE · LONDON

First published in Great Britain 1997

ISBN 0 7090 5978 7

Robert Hale Limited
Clerkenwell House
Clerkenwell Green
London EC1R 0HT

2 4 6 8 10 9 7 5 3 1

The reference to Alan Thompson promoting the work of Alexander Vorobyov (on the inside back flap of the jacket) may not now be current.

Photoset in North Wales by
Derek Doyle & Associates, Mold, Flintshire.
Printed in Great Britain by
St Edmundsbury Press Ltd, Bury St Edmunds, Suffolk.
Bound by WBC Book Manufacturers Limited,
Bridgend, Mid-Glamorgan.

Contents

Acknowledgements

I wish to extend my thanks to Duncan Hislop of the Art Sales Index Ltd for supplying Figures 1–5 and to Shire Publications Ltd for permission to use material based on extracts from *Discovering Antique Prints* by Ronald Russell.

The books listed in the bibliography have provided me with information and advice which have been of considerable assistance in the preparation of this book and which I gratefully acknowledge. I would also like to thank the many people in the trade from whom I have learnt so much.

Introduction

You have viewed the painting you want to buy, marked it in the catalogue, and waited with increasing expectation, and perhaps trepidation, for the auctioneer to reach your number.

'Lot No. 172, the Bloggs – *A View from the Bridge*. What shall we start this at? £500?'

Silence.

'£300 then.'

Silence.

'I don't mind. £200 then?'

Your heart leaps. You are prepared to pay £400 for it. You wave your hand, but several others have waved theirs.

'220.' '250.' '280.' '300.' '320.' '350.' '380.' '400.' '450.'

'450. Any advance on 450? The bid is with the lady in the middle.' And the auctioneer looks at you. '450,' he repeats. 'Well, if there are no more bids ...' He hesitates, looks round the room. Silence prevails. 'Bang' goes the gavel. You have bought a picture. He looks at you. You hold up your paddle, and he makes a note of the number.

Now you wonder whether you should have waved that final time, whether you should have raised your bid from £380 to £450. Why were you so anxious to have the picture? You are vaguely aware you paid more than you intended, which vagueness rapidly evaporates when you add on the buyer's premium and the VAT on the premium and realize it has cost you £529 altogether.

You pay and queue to collect quite a large water-colour. As soon as it is handed over, you can see that it is foxed and has slight burn marks. Also, the frame is more damaged than it seemed to be yesterday when you viewed it.

But you have an old water-colour – hopefully Victorian – by Bloggs.

A voice behind you says, 'He ran you up on that one.'

'Did he?' you say wonderingly.

'Not half – against the wall from £300.'

'Oh, but I like it.'

'That's alright then, but it needs money spent on it.'

'Yes, I suppose so.'

'I can take those marks out for fifty quid. Here's my card. Oh, and another thirty for reframing.'

'Thank you very much.'

'You're welcome'. And he of the old pullover and unshaved face mooches off to his BMW.

As you sidle out of the auction room, you bump into a friend.

'Look at this,' he says, 'twenty quid, and everyone missed it. It's worth 400 in London.'

'A bit rough on whoever put it into auction,' you comment.

Clearly it is all too easy to pay too much when you buy, and to get too little when you sell.

It is possible to make money buying and selling pictures – on a continuing basis or over the long run – but it is not as simple as it looks. 'Buy what you like' is good advice if you just want something pleasant to hang on your wall. Trading profitably requires many more considerations, price clearly being the basic one. But there are many other factors, including the reputation of the artist, the subject-matter, aesthetic appeal, commercial attraction, the condition, the frame and its authenticity. Then there are the rules and practices of the market-place – the auction houses, galleries, fairs, exhibitions, car boot sales and the private sales.

It has been said that dealing on the Stock Exchange and betting on racehorses are relatively safe and unspeculative activities compared to buying and selling pictures. In northern India, what looks like a pleasant English wood is actually full of tigers, leopards, wild elephants and cobras. The world of picture-dealing is also a deceptively friendly looking jungle where money, rather than life, is at risk.

Dealing in pictures is a lifelong study, which is both interesting and exciting. In common with most skills, it can only be learnt the hard way, but the purpose of this guide is to help you to avoid a good deal of disappointment and frustration.

1 Price and Value

The Price of Pictures

This book is about not paying over the odds when you buy pictures and not being fleeced when you sell them. By 'pictures', is meant oil paintings, water-colours, prints and drawings. The book is not unconcerned about value, but it is predominantly concerned with price. Oscar Wilde said, 'a cynic is a man who knows the price of everything and the value of nothing'. Our aim should be to know the market price of what we want to buy and sell and the value of the works to us and to our prospective purchasers.

I remember buying an odd lot of paintings and drawings at auction. As the sale was coming to an end, a very agitated man approached me and told me that one of the drawings I had bought had been slipped into the lot by mistake and was a drawing by his daughter and of great sentimental value. For a drawing that in terms of auction prices was worth nothing, he offered me nearly as much as I had paid for the whole lot. He would have paid a great deal more if I had haggled with him. Value was everything to him; price didn't matter.

The price of pictures is an intriguing subject. Why was it that van Gogh sold only one painting in his lifetime but some people are now prepared to pay millions of pounds for one of his works? An unsigned painting might sell at auction for very little and subsequently, if the experts have decided it is by a well-known artist – for example, John Constable – its price shoots up into hundreds of thousands of pounds. The painting hasn't changed, only the attribution. The price is decided by supply and demand, which, in turn, is determined not so much by the intrinsic worth of the picture, as it is by marketing. Some modern art is so obviously rubbish that when one sees it fetching telephone numbers at auction, one feels like the child in the fairy tale about the emperor's new clothes. One might acknowledge that a painting by van Gogh is better than one by Harold Harvey ... but 1,000 times better?

Robert Wraight put it coldly in his book *The Art World*: 'A painting has no intrinsic worth. It is a luxury commodity for which a market is deliberately created and maintained by financially interested parties, who are neither more nor less noble than the operators of any other legal market.'

What is the Right Price?

What is the right price for a picture? Is it what you would have to pay in a gallery, what you would pay at auction or what you might pick it up for in a car boot sale?

Many people currently form their ideas as to prices from the British television programme *The Antiques Road Show*. The way prices are quoted on the show illustrates the confusion that can arise. For instance, for a particular item an expert will say, 'That should fetch [so much] at auction.' For another, 'You would have to pay so much for that at a good picture gallery'. And for yet another, 'You should insure it for such and such an amount.' These prices for a particular picture vary considerably. The picture that fetches £5,000 at auction will probably appear in a West End gallery priced at £12,500 and, when bought, should be insured for £17,500.

Probably the most realistic price is the auction price, but

auction prices depend on a number of factors, as will become apparent in chapters 6 and 7. To illustrate this point, some dealers make a living out of buying at one auction to sell at a profit at another one. For example, a dealer might buy in Cornwall a painting by an artist who worked in Scotland, in the hope that he can put it into an auction in Scotland and thereby make a good profit. To do this successfully, the 'hammer' price in Scotland would have to be something like 50 per cent more than it was in Cornwall. Other dealers, who are often what the trade calls 'runners', buy at auction to sell to galleries. The 'real' price is therefore sometimes higher than a particular auction price, but sometimes it can be lower. Nevertheless, with a few caveats, auction prices are probably a better guide than anything else.

If this is accepted, then it is clear that, in commercial picture-dealing terms, whatever one pays for most amateur work at the church bazaar or the annual exhibition of the local art society, is money down the drain. In value terms it may be a different story. This is also true for much contemporary work by professional or semi-professional artists. Try selling their original works of art at auction and this will immediately become apparent. You may advertise them and be lucky enough to find a collector. Or you may sell to a dealer, but he is unlikely to pay more than a third of what he might hope to sell them for, and, if they won't sell at auction, that is not likely to be very much.

There are, of course, exceptions, and there are a number of contemporary painters who can command high prices for their work and can see them realized at auction. For example, an R.B. Kitaj painting – interestingly entitled *Value, Price and Profit* – sold for £220,000 at Sotheby's London in 1994. But present-day painters who can command modest prices at auction are probably less than 1 per cent of those actively working and exhibiting. Much of what the rest paint is uncommercial, although, more than likely, beautiful and inspired. If you buy their works, it must be because you like them or you want to support a charity or help a struggling young artist. Perhaps you are a friend or a relation of the artist or you think you are clever enough to have spotted a potential van Gogh in an early stage of development. These are all very good reasons, but only the last one has a grain of commercial sense.

The same is true of most of the prints sold in furniture shops – the resale price is virtually zero. There are prints that are worth a lot of money – everyone is familiar with signed prints by Sir William Russell Flint, many of which are worth hundreds of pounds. Some lithographs by Marc Chagall sell for thousands. But go to auctions and see what prints fetch – some, a hundred or two, most a few pounds and decorative prints (known in the trade as 'furnishing prints') nothing.

Buy What You Love or be Hard-headed?

Many proprietors of antique shops or art galleries will tell you to buy what you will be happy to have on your wall and not to be too concerned about price or appreciation. In other words, they are focusing your attention on value rather than on price. If you ask why a particular picture carries such-and-such a price, you may be told that the artist is very collectable or that the picture is an important one or in 'the books'. What 'books'? If you press the point, it is possible you will be shown a price book. Make sure it is the most recent one, not one dated 1988 when prices were particularly high.

However, there is some merit in the advice to buy what you like. This is where investment in pictures differs from that in stocks and shares. Whilst you have a picture that you love, you are getting value from it. The same cannot be said for a share certificate. And if the price falls to zero, the shares have no value but you still have your picture, even if no one wants to buy it.

If what you like corresponds to what your potential purchasers are going to like, you are on sound ground and can develop a 'nose' for a picture. Nevertheless, there are a considerable number of factors to take into account if you are to buy and sell successfully. Your personal preference is likely to be overridden when you have the opportunity to buy a picture you don't particularly like, at a fraction of the price at which you can sell it.

Market Trends

As the financial services people say, 'Prices can fall as well as rise'. In the broadest sense, prices tend to follow the economic cycles of boom and recession. Booms engender over-confidence and have often been encouraged by low

Fig. 1 Value & Volume Trends

World Art Auction Market

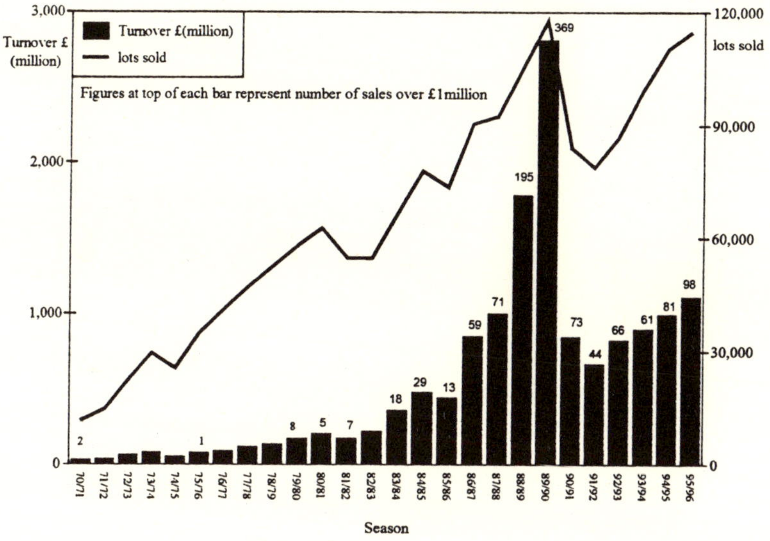

interest rates. In the art world, ever-increasing prices for a range of artists, such as the Impressionists, lead to more and more people wanting to get into the rising market, which for a while is propelled by this excessive optimism. Suddenly – and it generally *is* suddenly – governments are forced, by fear of rising inflation, to raise interest rates. Soon confidence begins to wain. Whilst prices are going up, the interest costs of holding stock can be ignored. With interest rates going up and prices starting to falter, it begins to look prudent to start selling. Soon, the factors driving the market up reverse, and the market plummets.

This is what happened in 1990/91 (see fig. 1 above). The effect has been dramatic, particularly where Japanese purchases are concerned. For example, Joan Miró's *Les Echelles en roue de feu traversant l'azur* was bought in 1990 for $7.15 million, including commission, but subsequently, when sold in November 1994, made only $1.9 million, with

Fig. 2 Value & Volume Trends

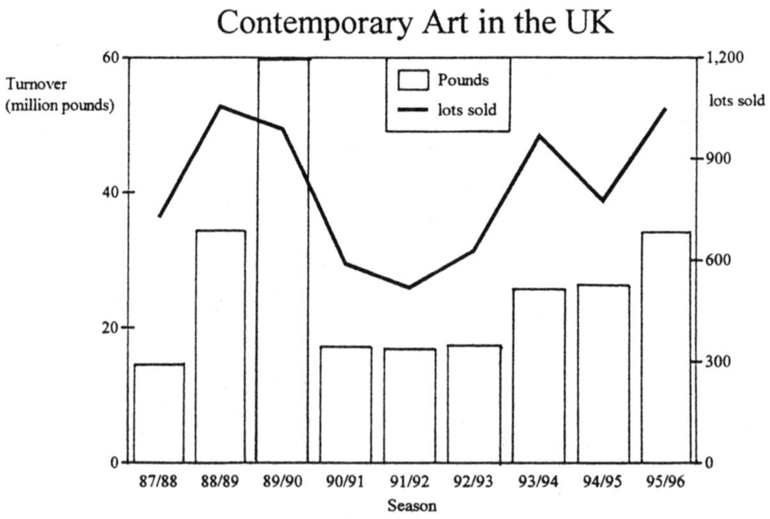

sales commission still to be paid. The effect of such a bust can be felt for years, as items are filtered back into the market as soon as the market attempts to rise.

Within this broad economic cycle, there can be secondary movements in particular categories of art. None of any significant size evaded the dramatic downturn, but some have recovered more quickly than others. For example, contemporary art in the UK has recovered well, but not in the USA. (See figs. 2 and 3.)

Fig. 3 Value & Volume Trends

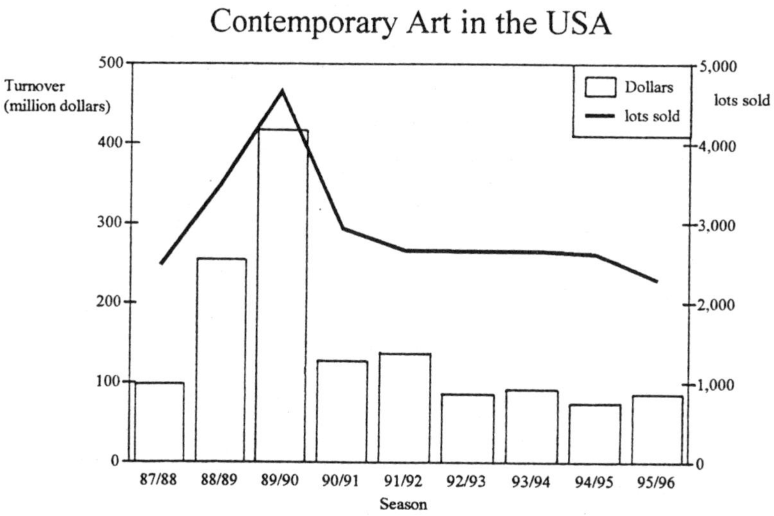

Within art categories, there are schools of artists such as the Newlyn School of artists who painted in and around Newlyn in Cornwall. The movement in total value and number sold at auction is shown in fig. 4. It can be seen that there was a build-up of interest during the latter part of the 1980s followed by a horrendous drop and a very halting, if at all existent, recovery. Average prices show a less dramatic rise and fall. The chart could be interpreted as indicating that 1997 could be a good time to buy Newlyn School paintings.

Fig. 4 Value & Volume Trends

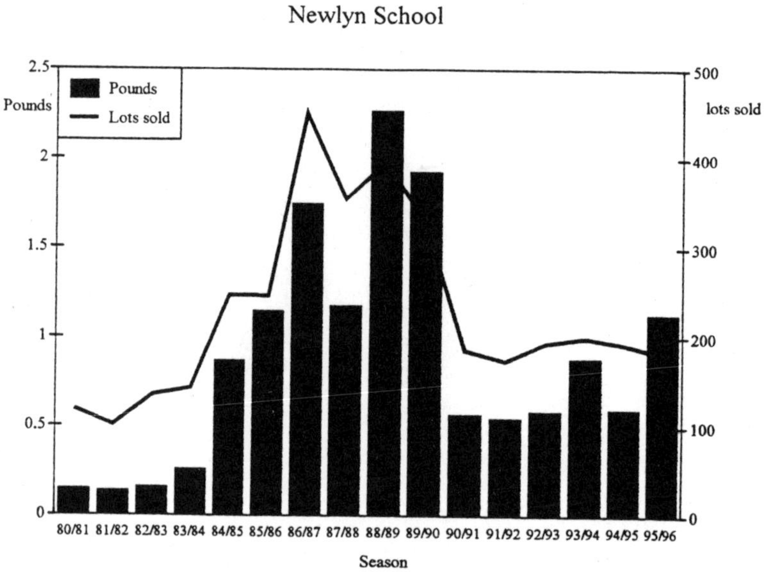

Finally, there is the individual artist. Fig. 5 opposite shows a similar chart for the contemporary British painter, Terry Frost – again a rise and fall with no recovery in volume, although average prices have been fairly stable since 1990/91.

Fig. 5 Value & Volume Trends

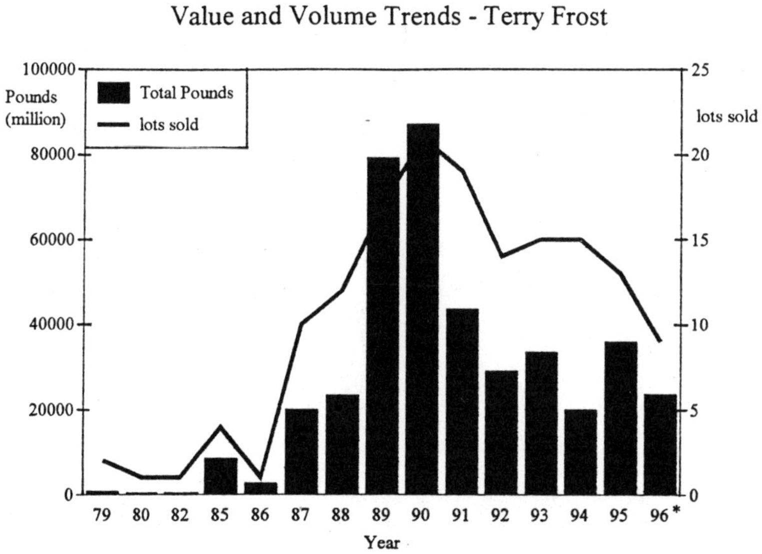

* as at 30 October

Year of Sale	*Number sold*	*lowest*	*Prices average*	*highest*	*Total Value*
1979	2	200	450	700	900
1980	1	230	230	230	230
1982	1	300	300	300	300
1985	4	820	2,155	5,000	8,620
1986	1	2,800	2,800	2,800	2,800
1987	10	504	2,010	4,500	20,104
1988	12	380	1,956	4,800	23,480
1989	17	700	4,661	16,000	79,250
1990	21	470	4,153	14,000	87,220
1991	19	420	2,304	8,200	43,780
1992	14	350	2,085	5,500	29,190
1993	15	420	2,241	5,500	33,620
1994	15	320	1,342	5,500	20,130
1995	13	600	2,773	18,000	36,050
1996	9	500	2,650	5,500	23,850
Total	154	200	2,659	18,000	409,524

Art Sales Index exercise great care in the recording and presentation of art auction prices but can accept no responsibility for errors or omissions.

Superimposed on all this are changes of fashion – for example, the surge of interest in paintings of cats – and the actions of the prestigious galleries in promoting the works of a particular artist. Why one artist takes off and another does not cannot often be discerned in terms of the intrinsic worth of the artist. It is often largely a question of supply and demand coupled with a conviction that pictures by the artist will appreciate in price. Artists that were waxing in 1995 were Robert Oscar Lenkiewicz, Sir William Russell Flint, Sir Alfred Munnings, David Shepherd and Laurence Stephen Lowry, whilst those whose value was waning include Marcel Dyf and – at the top end – Vincent van Gogh, Anders Zorn and Tsugouharu Foujita.

Art Sales Index Ltd (ASI) publish *Art Market Bulletin*, to which the charts in figs. 1-5 are attributable. This provides a number of graphs of value in dollars and lots sold, together with valuable reports on markets in the UK and overseas.

Price Books and Data Banks

The *Art Sales Index* (ASI) is one of the most popular and useful of price books. The current issue (1995/1996), in two volumes, covers sales of over 112,500 works of art from 390 auctioneers around the world. It deals with drawings, water-colours, oils, miniatures and sculpture.

Each entry gives the artist's name, dates of birth and death and nationality, the price of the work of art realized in pounds sterling and American dollars, the title or description of the picture, dimensions (height and width in centimetres and inches), whether it is signed and/or dated, the support and medium (if not oil on canvas), date of auction, auctioneer and place of sale, lot number of picture and whether it is illustrated in the sale catalogue, and estimates.

Art Sales Index Ltd also supplies a CD-ROM covering the period 1990–6 – 640,000 auction sales by 95,000 artists who sold at 13,000 auctions from 580 auction houses. At the other end of the scale, ASI also publishes a cheaper and smaller *Picture Price Guide* with, currently, 30,000 prices summarized from 693 auctions by 102 auctioneers in the UK. This is a useful guide to carry around in the back pocket.

A similar compilation is Mayer's *International Auction Records* which lists 80,000 auction prices from more than 2,400 international sales. In addition to drawings, water-colours, paintings and sculpture, it also covers prints.

What claims to be the largest annual art price guide is 1996 *The Art Price Index*. This lists 200,000 auction results – sold or not sold. It is the only price guide that includes art that was withdrawn from auction or did not sell. It gives 30,000 print results in addition to those for watercolours, drawings, oils and photographs.

There are no illustrations in the Art Sales Index or the 1996 Art Price Review International and only a smattering of them in Mayer. The *Lyle Paintings Price Guides* are full of illustrations but are considerably less comprehensive. The 1994 edition runs to 607 pages and, with about four illustrations to a page, covers about 2,500 paintings – water-colours and oils – with prices for each. Unfortunately, the 1994 *Picture Price Guide* was the last one to be published, so that second-hand bookshops and book sales are now the only way to get copies. Miller's also produces an illustrated price guide, the 1996 *Miller's Picture Price Guide*, which has 4,000 illustrations, 400 in colour. There is also a 1994 *Print Price Index* with 50,000 entries from 440 auctions. There are no 1995 or 1996 editions.

All of the above guides – which are typical, although there are a number of others – appear annually so that keeping up to date is quite an expensive business.

Bear in mind that all the above price books quote the hammer price at which the picture is sold or bought in. To arrive at what the picture costs, you have to add on the buyer's premium and the VAT on the buyer's premium, which together may be as much as an extra 17.62 per cent.

An alternative is to subscribe to a data bank. For example, the ASI Enquiry Service, Art Quest, contains details of over 1.65 million works of art sold at 40,000 auctions world-wide since 1970. New entries are made at the rate of 90,000 entries per year. For a fee, one can have access to this mass of information. Questions can be asked by telephone, fax or letter. Art Quest On-line Data Base enables the same data base to be interrogated through a PC (personal computer) and modem. This enables one to browse, i.e. make a series of enquiries. A typical search can be completed in two minutes and the data base can be accessed twenty-four hours a day, seven days a week.

Thesaurus is another service with a major data bank which accesses about 10,000 lots from more than forty catalogues daily. It is a before-the-event service. Subscribers inform Thesaurus what they are looking for – an artist, subject, country etc. They are then informed about relevant auctions to come. Each print-out shows the name and address of the sale room, date and time of the auction, telephone and fax numbers, contact name and a full lot description with its relevant number. Estimates are shown. Information is provided by post, fax or on-line. It also provides commentaries on the markets, art news, and auction and exhibition calendars.

Christie's have a lot finder service which will scan the text of almost every Christie's catalogue in the world, for a particular item. If it finds an item that matches your requirements, it will send you the lot description together with details of the specialist in charge of the sale, the telephone number and forms to order a catalogue or leave a bid.

Estimating a Price

The price books have to be used with caution when

estimating the price of a picture. If you look up a particular artist you will see that there is quite a wide range of values. First, make sure to distinguish whether you are looking at oils or water-colours. Next try to match the picture you are interested in with some of those in the book – as to size, subject, date and, if not an oil, the type of media, i.e. pencil and water-colour, pencil heightened with bodycolour, pastel, etc. Note that there is a lower value below which the picture will not appear in the list – for ASI in 1995/6 this was £400 for oils and £350 for works on paper, and for the 1966 Art Price Index International, starting prices ranged from 500 to 2,000 US dollars.

If one is able to view the picture before an auction, there are a number of aspects to consider that are dealt with in later chapters. You will also be able to discover the auctioneer's estimate. If this is much lower than what you have estimated from your research into the price books, there are a number of possible explanations: the subject-matter is boring and uncommercial; the auctioneer has failed to recognize the importance of the artist; the auctioneer hopes to entice potential bidders by a low estimate; or there is something wrong with the picture. If the auctioneer's estimate is much higher than your researched figure, it may be that the subject is exceptionally interesting, or that the quality is outstanding.

Summary

This preliminary discussion of price and value has attempted to distinguish between a commercial price and the 'I don't care what it costs. I like it and I want it' value price. Every one who puts anything into auction hopes that two buyers will turn up, each with a value judgement rather than a commercial one, and will fight each other to the death.

The commercial price is difficult to assess. Biographies and price guides help, but many factors affect the value of a work of art, as is discussed in subsequent chapters. If it were easy, everyone would be making a fortune as a picture dealer. Some, who are either very clever or very lucky or both, are very rich. Most win some and lose some and hope that occasionally they will spot a picture of considerable value – at auction or elsewhere – that no one else recognizes.

2 Sources of Information about Artists

An important part of buying and selling pictures successfully is to get to know the artists. There are so many that have painted or are presently painting, that it is clearly impossible to know them all. You need therefore to concentrate on a few artists at first and to see as much of their work as possible.

However, faced with a catalogue for a picture auction, the artists on your short list may not appear at all. Nevertheless, it may be evident, upon viewing, that there are a number of pictures of charm and quality. If the pictures are signed or appear in the catalogue, you can look them up in the price books. If you cannot find any entries in the price books or you want to become better informed, then it is necessary to seek other sources of information.

So you need as much information as possible on a few artists; and sources of information on a great many artists – other than the price books. The names and addresses, telephone and fax numbers etc. for all the sources mentioned in this chapter are listed in Appendix 1.

The Biographical Books

There are a number of books which give biographical

details of artists. These enable you to discover whether an artist is 'known' and what sort of work is typical of him or her. They do not concern themselves with prices.

The most widely used book is *The Dictionary of British Artists – 1880–1940*, volume 5 of *The Dictionary of British Art* published by the Antique Collectors' Club Ltd. It is a compilation of 41,000 artists by J. Johnson and A. Greutzner. It gives the artist's name, the type of art in which he or she specialized, bibliographical details and the galleries and societies in which he or she exhibited. If an artist painting in this period is in this book, it does indicate that his or her work has been exhibited.

Perhaps a greater distinction is a listing in *The Dictionary of Victorian Painters* by Christopher Wood, volume 4 of *The Dictionary of British Art*. This covers the period from *c*. 1820 to 1914, and the information given is a little more fulsome than that in volume 5. It contains about 11,000 names and there is some overlap with volume 5. There is a second volume to *The Dictionary of Victorian Painters* called *Historical Survey and Plates* with forty-seven colour plates and 759 black-and-white illustrations.

The other volumes in the series are: *The Dictionary of 16th- & 17th-century British Painters* (volume 1), *The Dictionary of British 18th-century Painters in Oils and Crayons* (volume 2) and *20th-century Painters and Sculptors* (volume 6).

The Dictionary of British Watercolour Artists up to 1920 by H.L. Mallalieu is a valuable source containing biographical details of nearly 5,000 artists. Also important is *The Royal Watercolour Society: The First 50 Years, 1805–1855* (volume 1) which lists 17,000 water-colours exhibited at the RWS annual shows. There are also three volumes covering British portrait painters and a number of other volumes covering many other subjects, such as sporting scenes, marinescapes, botanical studies and illustrations. *British Prints: Dictionary and Price Guide* by Ian Mackenzie is a useful book that provides biographies of British printmakers from 1650 to 1950, as well as some price guides, which, incidentally, tend to be on the low side. All of the above may be obtained through the Antique Collectors' Club, as well as a book catalogue from the club at the address given in Appendix 1.

Another useful compilation is the *Dictionary of British Artists, Working 1900–1950* by Grant M. Waters. This is in two volumes, the first of which contains biographies of 5,500 artists, whilst the second has a further 1,100 biographies and illustrations of the works of nearly 400 artists. For listings of more contemporary artists there is *Who's Who in Art*, which includes nearly 3,000 names and more than 500 signatures. *Dictionnaire critique et documentaire des peintres, sculpteurs, dessinateurs et graveurs* by E. Bénézit is claimed to be the world's most complete and up-to-date biographical dictionary. The text is in French, and there are approximately 300,000 entries in the latest edition. Not to be outdone, the Germans have produced *Allgemeines Lexikon der bildenden Künstler von der Antike bis zur Gegenwart* (known as Thieme–Becker), supposed to be the largest biographical dictionary of artists from early history to the beginning of the twentieth century. It is in nineteen volumes, supplemented by a further six volumes entitled *Allgemeines Lexikon der bildenden Künstler des XX. Jahrhunderts* (Vollmer) bringing it up to the late twentieth century. There are also dictionaries giving complete listings of artists who exhibited at the Royal Academy of Arts, the Royal Scottish Academy, the Royal Glasgow Institute of the Fine Arts and the Royal Hibernian Academy of Arts. *The Illustrators from 1780 to the Present Day* by Chris Beetles is another interesting series that has been published.

Museums, Galleries and Libraries

If you have decided to concentrate on one artist, a few of them, or a school, then you will probably want to do research on them. A literature search can be carried out at most public galleries, and the relevant books can often be borrowed or at least perused within the confines of the gallery library. If you live in London, or can get there easily, there is a wealth of information available. The major art galleries such as the Royal Academy, the National Gallery, the Tate Gallery, the National Portrait Gallery, the National Maritime Museum (Greenwich), the Imperial War Museum, the National Army Museum and the Victoria and Albert Museum all may exhibit artists in whom you may be interested and are sources of much expertise.

The Westminster Reference Library, on the third floor above the public library, is located just behind the National Gallery and is an invaluable storehouse of information on art. The library has 6,000 exhibition catalogues from all the major London galleries; catalogues date from after the Second World War, although earlier ones are on microfiche. There is a book stock of over 30,000 monographs on artist, as well as copies of *The Year's Art* from 1883, the Macmillan *Dictionary of Art*, and the *Art Index* which is on CD. The library also has nineteenth-century catalogues from the National Gallery in London, the Metropolitan Museum in New York and the Fogg Museum at Harvard University, Cambridge, Massachusetts. And, as advertisers are wont to say, much, much more. It is worth a day's browsing.

The other remarkable library open to the public is the Witt Library of the Courtauld Institute of Art, located in Somerset House at the Aldwych end of The Strand. It is a collection of photographs, reproductions and cuttings – mostly in black and white but some in colour – of paintings, drawings and engravings of Western Art from about AD 1200 to the present day. The library contains over 1.8 million reproductions of the work of over 66,000 artists. The reproductions are arranged by national school and then by artist in alphabetical order. There is a Witt Computer Index – a data base which enables the information on the Witt mounts to be searched under various headings such as subject, location, provenance, etc. There are also a number of other indexes, including the Marburg Index microfiche of over half a million photographs of art in Germany.

In the UK, outside of London, there are many art galleries of national distinction. One that should be visited is the Ashmolean Museum in Oxford, where many wonderful pictures are exhibited and a great many more are available for inspection, provided arrangements are made in advance. Most major towns possess very fine art galleries. Smaller provincial museums and art galleries tend to specialize in the work of artists that lived in the region or painted locally. In most other industrialized countries the same sort of assistance and advice is provided – often free of charge – by institutions to people seeking further information about artists, and undertaking a little research can add interest to one's visit to a country and possibly provide a source of contacts and friends.

Clubs and Societies

The Antique Collectors' Club publishes a monthly magazine, *Antique Collecting*, which generally has at least one article devoted to paintings. It also publishes the various books dealing with art mentioned at the beginning of this chapter, and members have the opportunity to purchase new titles at pre-publication prices. The club also publishes details of many regional and specialist collectors' clubs, both in the UK and overseas. Telephone numbers of secretaries and costs of membership are given.

For a modest fee members of the public can become Friends of the Royal Academy. They receive an invitation to the private viewing of the Royal Academy Summer Exhibition, and they may attend this exhibition and other shows at the Academy throughout the year, free of charge. There is also a Members' Room where one can relax and enjoy a cup of coffee.

Magazines

The *Antiques Trade Gazette* is a weekly newspaper much patronized by the art trade. It contains a useful auction calendar listing auctions being held for each day of the week for about three weeks in advance. The listing is in alphabetical order by auctioneers' names. The town for each entry is shown in bold, which assists you to find auctions being held in your own area. *The Fine Art File* is a sort of newsletter designed for those interested in collecting nineteenth- and early twentieth-century paintings. It is published by Waterhouse & Dodd, whose main aim is to offer paintings for sale. *The File* is thus to some extent a catalogue, but it also provides guidance on buying pictures. Many paintings are illustrated in colour and are put into the context of the current market, with the price quoted. *The File* is available on a subscription basis.

There are a number of other magazines which are well worth buying or, at any rate, reading, if you can find a well-stocked library. Famous amongst these are *Apollo* – a sumptuous monthly devoted to the fine and decorative arts of all periods – and *Burlington Magazine*, which covers international exhibitions. The addresses, telephone and fax numbers of these and other magazines are listed in Appendix 1.

Catalogue Subscriptions

Nearly all auction houses issue catalogues ranging from plain photocopied sheets to the beautifully illustrated paper back books produced by major houses such as Sotheby's and Christie's, which are of considerable value and cost. Most auction houses encourage you to take out a subscription so that catalogues are posted to you ahead of sales.

There is also a trade in old catalogues. These can often be bought from auction houses – for example, Sotheby's sell their old catalogues in their entrance hall in London. Stalls at fairs often sell them. If one is a good customer of an auction house, it is possible that you may be lucky enough to receive catalogues free, but it is by no means a universal practice. If you have put pictures for sale at a particular auction, you will automatically be sent a catalogue for that sale.

Many galleries, both private and public, issue catalogues for which a charge is usual. A catalogue issued in connection with a major exhibition may be a definitive document for a particular artist or group and well worth buying.

Catalogues, particularly those with colour illustrations, are wonderful and relatively cheap sources of information, providing the opportunity to study many artists' works and to see the subjects they painted and the colours they used, as well as possibly being able to spot signatures and monograms.

The Internet

The Internet is one of those technological phenomena which at one time seemed irrelevant and therefore able to be ignored – and then suddenly became highly relevant, requiring urgent attention and understanding. It is a communications network already being used by more than 30 million people. In California, auctions are actually held on the Internet. Pictures of individual lots can be called up on your computer and you can bid. Bonhams provide information on forthcoming sales, extracts from catalogues and sale results on-line. Christie's, Phillips and Sotheby's offer similar information.

Independent of the main auction houses, at least one company – Corsellis-Montford-London – has been established to make facilities available for medium and smaller auction houses to promote their range of services and publish catalogues with high-resolution illustrations.

Another company, Desiderata (Interweb Systems) Ltd, has developed a sort of specialist antique and collector's mall.

To gain access to this burgeoning plethora of information on the Internet, you require a reasonably modern personal computer – perhaps a Pentium with eight megabytes of memory and with Windows installed – and a modem, which is a device to connect the computer with a telephone line. You also need an access provider, which is an organization that, for a single payment and a monthly fee, provides your modem with access to the Internet for the cost of a local telephone call.

The Internet also encompasses an electronic postal system: e-mail (electronic mail). This allows any computer to communicate with another computer using personalized electronic 'addresses'. It is now being recognized as being cheaper than a fax and enables dialogues to be set up with, for example, dealers world-wide. Increasingly, the e-mail address is now being put on sales literature along with the telephone and fax numbers.

For those active in buying and selling pictures, the Internet is highly relevant.

Electronic Catalogues

Electronic catalogues are a rapidly expanding area of activity, responding to the wide availability of modern computers of modest cost having CD-ROM players and access to the Internet via a modem. The following are two typical examples.

The *Art Review* has produced a CD-ROM which enables you to search for pictures and galleries in a range of categories including artist, medium, period/movement, schools and groups, style, price, nationality and genre. The CD-ROM automatically searches its data base and provides you with the names of suitable galleries. You can then visit a gallery 'on-screen', see the location and price and view up to forty examples of work in their collection.

Banca dell'Arte is a service supplying an electronic catalogue for artists, galleries, dealers and collectors. The service is a cross-referenced data base of pictures, galleries and artists who have subscribed to have images scanned and stored on Banca dell'Arte's computer. You can access this data base if you have an adequate computer – 486 with eight megabytes of RAM (random-access memory) and modem 14400 speed – by installing software called Wintelligent, which is supplied free. It is claimed that this system is superior to systems that can only be viewed on the Internet in that it is faster, and because it is an enclosed on-line software-based system, e-mail can be sent easily. So you could, for example, send a private message to anyone displaying their services, and they in turn could respond.

Summary

The scope for researching pictures and artists is inexhaustible and is one of the great fascinations of buying and selling pictures; you are never going to run out of topics to study. The material and sources available are equally extensive, and those mentioned in this chapter are merely in the nature of an hors d'oeuvre. You will find it advantageous to build up a basic library to which you can refer at short notice to supplement the price books. Some dealers, for example, carry the basic core of their library around with them in a box in the back of the car.

3 Setting out the Stall – What is on Offer

If you attend a general picture auction sale, you will often be surprised by the wide range of pictures on offer. Prints, drawings, water-colours and oils are the broad categories, and within these are many variants. As a collector, occasional trader or full-time dealer, you may specialize in one of these categories, just as you might specialize in a particular artist or subject – or you may decide to have a go at anything you like, have researched and seems good value at the price you are prepared to pay.

Prints

Prints are for the most part made on paper in such a way that a number of copies (impressions) can be made. Printing involves a printing surface, such as wood, copper or steel, on which a design is delineated in some way, ink and a printing press.

Some prints can be worth many thousands of pounds; others may be worthless. They can be obtained at auction or from specialist print dealers and are often to be seen on the walls of antique shops. Before the invention of photography, prints were the principal way of disseminating images of original oils and watercolours to those who could not afford the originals. Then, as now, many artists made or commissioned prints, which were often signed and were in limited editions with each print numbered serially or with an alphabetical code. This often enabled them to obtain more income from the prints than from the original painting.

Many prints have a good deal of information on them: the title of the picture; the name of the artist which is often indicated by the letters *del* meaning 'drew this'; the name of the person who made the print, e.g. the engraver; the process used; and often the publisher and the date of the print. Some Latin abbreviations used on prints, are listed in Ronald Russell's book, *Discovering Antique Prints*:

> Usually on the bottom left of the print – *del, delt, delin, descripsit, desig, designavit, inv., invenit* – all mean delineated, designed, drawn or invented. *Pinx, pinxit, ping, pingebat* mean painted. All these terms refer to the artist, which may be the original artist or an artist who copied the painting of a famous artist.
>
> Abbreviations, usually on the bottom right, refer to the engraver – *aqua, aquafort* means etched: *aquantinta* means engraved in aquatint; *F., fecit, faciebat* means made by; *inc, incidit, incidebat* means engraved; *lith., lithog.* means lithographed; *sc., sculp., sculpsit, sculpebat* means engraved.

Printing by Relief Processes

The woodcut or linocut is an example of a relief process. The wood block or linoleum block is cut in such a manner that the areas to be blank (i.e. those that will not be inked) are cut away, leaving the remainder (the inked areas) standing out in relief. In wood engraving, boxwood is often used, which is hard; it is worked with a burin, a sharp metal tool with a burred over end. Chiaroscuro woodcuts were made by using several woodblocks to print different colours.

Printing by Intaglio Processes

Intaglio processes involve incising the design into a metal plate. The plate is inked and the uncut areas are wiped clean. The plate is then pressed on to the paper, forcing the paper into the incisions to take up the ink. The edge of the plate makes an indentation all round the paper's edge.

In line engraving, the engraver draws lines on a copper or steel plate with a burin. If the print is earlier than 1821, it is likely to have been made from a copper plate. After that date, steel began to replace copper. In copper engravings, the parallel lines are further apart than in a steel engraving, and the line looks heavier.

In etching, the metal plate is covered with wax into which the design is drawn with an etching needle. The plate is put into an acid bath which eats into the plate where the lines have been drawn. To obtain tonal variation, parts of the plate may be varnished and then put into the acid again. This may be repeated a number of times.

Aquatint is a method of etching to simulate water-colours and wash drawings. A powdered resin is sprinkled on to a heated plate. According to the density of the particles, subsequent immersion in acid causes tonal variations to be produced. Outlines are etched in before or after the application of the resin or put in by drypoint. Often they were printed in black and white and coloured by hand with water-colour.

Drypoint is the incising of the line directly into the copper plate with a strong needle. The burr is left on the plate and results in a rich black tone when printed.

In the mezzotint process the plate is worked over with a spiked rocker until the whole surface is roughened. Areas of the plate are then scraped and smoothed. The process relies on shade and tone rather than outline and was widely used in the seventeenth century to create portraits.

Lithographs, Mechanical Prints, Silk Screen Prints and Oleographs

Lithography is based on repulsion of water by grease. The design is drawn with a waxy lithographic crayon on a porous stone, such as limestone. The stone is then soaked in water, which is repelled by the greased surfaces. The ink used has a greased base and will adhere only to the drawn lines. Paper is laid on to the stone, and the design is transferred. There is no indentation or plate mark with a lithograph. Generally, old lithographs were printed in black and coloured by hand. Chromolithographs were popular in the late nineteenth century and are lithographs printed in colour by using a series of stones, one for each colour. They can be confused with water-colours but may be distinguished from them by looking at the colours and registration, as well as the paper, which has a bobbled appearance. Before the invention of chromolithography, most prints were coloured by hand, either when the print was issued or at a later date.

Mechanical prints can be seen in abundance, often expensively framed, in department stores and furniture shops. Inspected with a magnifying glass, the small dots of colour can instantly be seen. With a little experience, the difference between a water-colour and a mechanical print of a water-colour can be spotted with the unaided eye. However, it should be noted that some car boot finds thought at first to be prints have actually turned out to be genuine water-colours. Mechanical prints are produced in limited edition – for example, some prints by Beryl Cook – and are signed by the artist, giving them some sort of cachet and resulting in a price many times that of an unsigned print.

Silk screen prints are made by using a finely meshed screen, often of silk, and stencils to transfer the image to the paper. Limited edition prints are often supervised by the artist, and each print is to some extent a one-off. They are signed by the artist and numbered or lettered, and some artists' prints can appreciate considerably with time.

Oleographs are pictures printed in oil-colour inks to look like an oil painting. Some of them are quite convincing, if one does not examine them too closely.

Drawings

Over the years drawings have been done using various materials. Pencil is what immediately comes to mind, and some pencil drawings by famous artists are of considerable value. Pen-and-ink drawings have existed since ancient times, those by Rembrandt being the best known. Often pen-and-ink is combined with wash in a drawing. Charcoal is probably the oldest drawing material and is widely used by students at art colleges and by professional artists for both rough sketches and finished drawings. Charcoal smudges readily and needs to be fixed.

Chalks were popular in the Renaissance period when white and red chalks were often used to heighten pen-and-ink drawings. Conté chalks have been used since 1795 and are now available in a variety of colours. Crayon bound with wax is often the first medium a child will use, but some professionals, particularly illustrators, use it as well. Pastels are drawn – or, some might say, painted – with sticks of dry colour which have a minimum of binder. It is essential that pastel drawings are fixed, otherwise particles of colour will detach from the paper and smudge.

Water-colours

Water-colours are generally on paper, and, strictly speaking, the pigment is translucent so that light is reflected from the paper underneath. The water-colour artist has to commit himself with each mark of the brush. It requires a high degree of skill to produce the effect of light and of immediacy which characterizes a good water-colour.

Gouaches, on the other hand, are painted with opaque pigments mixed with gum, and they allow the opportunity to work a painting up, to cover over mistakes and to make changes. Water-colours are sometimes 'heightened' with white body-colour, i.e. white gouache; other gouache colours may also be used. The term 'mixed media' means a technique in which two or more media are used to create a picture.

Oil Paintings

The support of an oil painting is usually a canvas or board, and the paint consists of pigments mixed with oils, e.g. linseed oil or poppy oil. Before oil paints were developed in the fifteenth century, pigments were mixed with egg yolk in a technique called tempera. Tempera paintings continue to be produced into the late twentieth century.

Summary

There are a great many products on the world-wide picture stall, a fact often reflected in the variety evident at a good picture auction sale. Each medium used and image produced is the result of considerable technical skill and knowledge. There are many variations in each, and many books are devoted to a single category, such as lithography, for example. The advice to specialize seems relevant, so that you can become an expert in part of the field.

4 First Thoughts on Buying and Selling

Buying is Easier than Selling

Generally, buying comes before selling, but it is possible that you may have inherited some pictures or found some in the attic and are thinking of selling without having had any experience of buying. Clearly, buying is easier, both psychologically and in actuality, than selling. For many people buying pictures is an addiction – like smoking or betting on horses. They cannot avoid the lure of an auction or any other kind of sale and, once there, they have to buy. With selling there are mental barriers – always the possibility – or, more realistically, the probability of refusal; also there is the fear that you are selling too cheaply or too soon.

When I first decided that I wanted to deal in pictures, I asked the advice of a well-known gallery owner. He said, 'Attend fifty auctions before you think of buying anything.' This was excellent advice, and I wish that I had taken it. However, it is rather like saying to an intending horse-race punter, 'Attend fifty race meetings before you place a bet.' Furthermore, it is only when you start putting money on that you really learn. The pain of making a foolish purchase, of paying too much or buying unsaleable rubbish, has to be felt before one gains sense. Also one realizes that 'one swallow does not make a summer'. It is easy to think, if you have made a good purchase, that you have got the subject of art dealing licked. The next auction teaches you that you haven't.

Selling is the real testing time, when you discover whether or not you have been clever. Making a profit is an exquisite experience. Selling at a loss is a misery, and not selling at all is a disaster. That is, until you realize that 'you win some and you lose some' – and that this applies not only to you but to everyone else in the business.

Often a good time to buy at auction is when there are several sales at the same time in the same locality. Hopefully, many of the dealers will be elsewhere so that the competition is lessened. Equally, a good time to sell is when there is only one sale in the district.

Both buying and selling are influenced, to a greater or lesser extent, by fear and greed – unless money is no object. It is a pity, but nevertheless a fact, that considerations of aesthetic and financial appreciation travel together, sometimes in harness and sometimes in opposition.

What and When to Buy

Before setting off to buy pictures, it is necessary to ask yourself: 'What are you hoping to achieve?' Many people start buying pictures and antiques and collectables from a mixture of impulses – *The Antiques Road Show*; the rapid increase in money terms of works of art; the wish to have something old and from another age; or the need to have something on the wall.

It may be that you would like to buy the present-day equivalent of a Cezanne painting, i.e. to buy for very little something that will become very valuable, because you have had the perception to see what others failed to see. Out of the multitude of unacknowledged artists painting today, one or two or maybe more will emerge as being highly valued.

This happened, for example, with Alfred Wallis, who began to paint at the age of 68, after his wife's death in 1922. Paintings that could have been picked up literally for a few shillings, now fetch a great deal of money. Spotting a future winner is probably many times more difficult than finding a needle in a haystack unless one has inside information. Exhibitions in private galleries can sometimes lead one to artists whose work is consistently commanding higher prices. Gallery owners are frequently agents for particular artists and have a considerable vested interest in seeing the prices achieved by their stable of artists appreciate.

Perhaps you want to be a collector of an individual artist or group of artists. To specialize in this way is sensible because you get to know a particular artist well – the subjects, the colours, the way he or she applied paint and the artist's signature. Do you want to collect the work of an established artist or of one who is as yet unrecognized? If the former, then there is plenty of information to guide you as to price, whereas with unknown artists, one is often in the dark.

Another impulse is to invest in art, to buy right across the range anything that seems to be a bargain so that it can be sold later at a profit. Investment can range from serious purchases with excellent provenances from reputable dealers to auction bids for something you think is valuable but which no one else has seen, that is from conservative investment to outright speculation. Some buyers make money on odds-on favourites, some on rank outsiders and many do neither.

There are at least three kinds of investors: the first wants to develop a cash flow and to buy and sell on a continuous basis. He has to find purchases that he can sell readily, and so where and how to sell is of prime importance. The second wants to buy for capital appreciation and to sell in the future as the need for funds arises. He needs to pick the work of established artists and subjects for which there appears to be a steady demand, so that problems do not occur when it is necessary to sell. The third is the investor for the long term – perhaps for his children. He can mix the safe and the speculative, rather like a portfolio of blue-chip and potentially high-flyer shares.

With a given amount of money to spend – say £10,000, or for that matter, £1,000 – you have the option of buying one picture, using the argument that you should 'always buy the very best you can', or you can buy several in order to spread your risk. The latter approach has the advantage that you have more pictures to hang on your walls and are less concerned with security, than if you have just one large investment showing off its virtues to an intruder.

Should you decide to put all your eggs in one basket, you have also to decide if you will hang it on the wall and enjoy it and give thought to security and insurance. Alternatively, you can incarcerate it in some vault, where it will give you no pleasure other than the possibility of capital appreciation.

What and When to Sell

Unless you are weeding out a collection or are giving up collecting or dealing in pictures, what to sell was really determined when you decided what to buy and then actually bought. So the remaining questions is: 'when to sell?' Over the past fifty years, the prices of pictures, as with most other works of art, have steadily gone up. Some older readers will remember how they could have bought an Alfred Munnings in the 1950s for two or three hundred pounds, which today might fetch £100,000. Buying pictures seemed as safe as buying houses – the price may not always go up, but it would never come down. However, prices of many pictures, as of houses, came down between 1988/9 and 1991/2. As with shares, there is a time to buy and a time to sell if you want to make money but, as with shares, it is not easy to pick the right time.

There was a massive wave of buying paintings of the Middle East – for example, scenes of Arabia – as the oil boom developed, and which receded as the price of oil subsequently fell. The incursion of Japanese business into the modern Impressionist art market led to exceptional prices being paid for paintings by van Gogh. *Portrait of Dr Gachet* sold for 82,500,000 US dollars to a Japanese dealer bidding on behalf of a Japanese company at Christie's, New York.

Where to Buy and Sell

The choices of where to buy and sell pictures include galleries, auctions, antique and junk shops, car boot sales and privately, i.e. answering advertisements or advertising for particular artists. All of these are covered in chapters 6–10.

Summary

Again, as was made clear in previous chapters, the attraction of the buying and selling pictures business is the fantastic variety – of prices, sources of information, of media and types of pictures, of subjects and artists – and, as this chapter emphasizes, the multiplicity of places where you can buy and sell and the need to get the timing right. You have to resist the temptation to rush about buying this and that, here and there. You need to think about how you are going to sell when you buy – unless you are buying for posterity.

5 Condition, Restoration, Framing and Fakes

Construction of Pictures

Structurally, a picture consists of two parts: a design or image, and a support (the material upon which the design or image is placed). Supports include stone, copper sheets, zinc sheets, leather, glass, terracotta and plaster, but the most common are wood, fabric and paper. The problem with wood is that it has a tendency to warp or split along the lines of the grain and to attract wood-boring insects. Linen is the most common fabric in the West, as is silk in the Far East. Both are treated with sizing materials, particularly animal glue, which shrinks and swells, gets brittle and grows mould when damp. There are two types of paper: rag paper, made from cotton or linen rags; and pulp paper, made from wood fibre. Ground-up pulp, which came into use in the late eighteenth century, discolours and mould grows on it readily.

A ground is a sort of plaster which is laid as a flat smooth coating on to the support. Ground may be of chalk, chalky substances such as gypsum, or china clay with a binder, usually a skin or animal glue. Oil grounds can be made with white lead or titanium white, often mixed with a chalky substance. Often glue is used to size a canvas and may be a source of deterioration. The paint is laid on the ground and consists of a powder pigment and a binding material. Many binding materials are in use – egg yolk, egg white and gum arabic – but oil is the most common. The oil has to be one which dries through chemical change and which is consequently subject to deterioration and brittleness.

To protect the surface of an oil painting, a varnish is applied. Many varnishes are resins, which tend to become brittle and darken with age.

Condition and Damage

General advice: The best advice that one can give to those inexperienced in assessing the condition of a work of art is to try to avoid pictures that are obviously damaged or in poor condition. It costs money to have them repaired and, in so doing, may render the picture worthless.

Prints: The quality of printing, i.e. the clarity and density of the impression, is obviously very important. Lack of this may indicate that the print is a re-strike, printed from an original plate but at a much later date than is indicated on the print. The colours of the print may have faded. This may be excusable in an older print but not in a twentieth-century one.

Blemishes on the surface may be due to the accumulation of dirt or grime. Stains can be caused by water or other liquids or may come from cardboard or wooden backboards. Brown spots of mould – foxing – can often be seen and is usually caused by dampness. Attention should also be given to tears in the paper, missing bits of paper and their locations on the print. Intaglio prints should have the impressed plate mark. There are many mechanical copies of old prints that have been put into old frames; these are worthless and can be detected by their lack of an impression. Prints may have had their edges cut off in order to fit them into a frame. This is unacceptable for a twentieth-century print but may be more acceptable in an older print, provided the plate mark impression is present.

A print should not be stuck down, as the adhesive may discolour the paper and the image. Ideally, to examine a print properly, it should be removed from its frame. As this is often not possible, one should exercise care and scepticism when judging the worth of the print.

Drawings: Much of what has been said about the condition of prints also applies to drawings. Additionally, damage in a drawing may be evident from abrasion or rubbing. If a charcoal drawing or a pastel is smudged, this means that it has either been inadequately fixed, or not at all.

Water-colours: Again, like drawings, water-colours can suffer from the same problems as prints. Foxing, scuffing and stains, particularly from wooden backboards, are common blemishes. Mould may be evident. Water-colours can fade quite quickly if exposed to bright sunlight. If the painting can be removed from the frame, the extent of fading can often be assessed by comparison with that part of the water-colour that has been covered up by the mount.

Oil paintings: Oil paint can suffer damage from many sources: scratches, drops of water, food and drink, and flies, the excrement of which is brown and acidic. Burns and scorching from fires, as well as the chemicals from fire extinguishers, can also be very damaging. Blemishes and deterioration can be caused by dust and grime; the darkening of the paint or varnish; or bloom, a sort of clouding which causes a loss of transparency.

Paintings frequently get scratched. This may only affect the varnish, or the scratch may go deeper into the paint and, possibly, the ground. The paint itself may crack or become detached from the ground, or both paint and ground may become detached.

Canvases can tear, and inspection of the back of a painting may reveal damage that has been repaired by patching.

Paintings that have suffered in this way are often lined. The nails holding the canvas on to the stretcher can rust and rot the canvas. If the canvas is very dry, the paint may be in the process of lifting away from the surface. This may be visibly apparent or may become evident if a fingertip is dragged across the back of the canvas.

Old paint shows its age by exhibiting craquelure, which is a network of cracks on the surface. The older the painting, the smaller the size of the cracks. If an old painting lacks craquelure, it has probably been overpainted.

Frames and stretchers can be riddled with woodworm. Wooden panels can warp and split, and paintings on such panels often exhibit cracks or fillings which become more obvious when you look at the back of the panel. Oil paintings on cardboard are liable to damage and should be mounted on wooden struts.

Restoration

Prints: Surface dust can be removed with a soft brush, and a soft eraser can be used to remove surface dirt. Foxing requires expert treatment (see *Water-colours* below). Prints which have been stuck on to a cardboard backing can be soaked to remove the backing. The restoration of valuable prints, including the repair of tears, requires the attention of a specialist – a paper conservator – who is an expert in the structure of paper and in the stabilizing of the acid content.

Water-colours: It is important to know what can be restored satisfactorily. A water-colour which has been kept out of the light, has been framed reasonably well and has good strength of colour can be readily restored, with the colour only being slightly affected. But a water-colour that is starting to show some signs of fading, may, if restored, end up with a very washed-out image, possibly making the work difficult to sell. Some restorers will 'touch-up' faded water-colours, and at times this will amount almost to a repainting.

A water-colour which has a little foxing is much easier to restore than a picture that has bad burn marks, i.e. tannin marks from wood that has been used as a backing (for example, from an old orange crate). These may not be able to be restored satisfactorily.

Problems can arise with water-colours that have been entirely painted, or even just heightened, with gouache or body-colour. They differ from transparent water-colours in that the pigments are bound with glue, and the lighter tones are obtained by the admixture of white pigment. The degree of opacity varies with the amount of white that is added but, in general, is sufficient to prevent the reflection of the paper through the paint. As a result, this type of painting lacks the luminosity of transparent water-colour painting. Furthermore, gouache or body-colour, being of a thicker consistency, tends to rest on top of the paper and does not totally bind with it. Therefore, it cannot be cleaned by the conventional methods used to clean water-colours. Sometimes the paint starts to lift, and it is very difficult to retouch. When it has been retouched, it is generally obvious that this has been done.

For pictures that are painted entirely in gouache or those that have a lot of body-colour or are heightened with white, specialist restoration work of the highest calibre is required. They are best avoided, unless the blemishes are acceptable or the picture is of such high monetary or sentimental value as to justify the high cost of restoration.

Oil Paintings: An oil painting on board may be bent or the paint may be flaking. If it is on a wooden panel, it is important that the panel should have been properly seasoned and that the wood is appropriate to the period. For example, if it is from the nineteenth century, it ought to be the right material, and if from the twentieth century, it should be the right manufacture (e.g. canvas over panel, dark grey academy board, fairly thick). Check to see that the painting has not been stretched on the back, in which case the ground – the gesso that holds the paint – will be affected.

An oil painting on canvas will be easier to restore if it is on an expensive canvas. If it is on a cheap canvas, it may need relining. There are two types of lining. Compo lining is a glue lining put on by heating the canvas at the back; wax lining has wax bonded between the old canvas and a new piece of canvas. The wax goes right through the ground to the underside of the paint and sucks the paint down on to the old canvas. The new canvas holds it secure, particularly if it has tears or breaks. It is important to be able to identify whether a picture has been lined and to be able to tell the difference between compo lining and wax lining, as this helps in estimating how long ago the painting was lined. Sometimes there is just a strip lining on the edge of the picture where it bends round the stretchers, and this can be easily missed. Many galleries in London's West End have all their pictures relined. However, it often makes the paintings look flat, and if relining is not done with care, much or all of the impasto can be lost.

Early nineteenth-century pictures with a bitumen base are affected by changes in temperature. Shrinkage takes place at a different rate than the paint. Large gaps in the paint appear, along with a discoloration from dark brown to almost a black. This is very difficult to restore and leaves a textured, mottled appearance. The cracks have to be filled either with a wash or with pigment on a 000 sable brush, which is very time-consuming. If the problem is in the sky and the picture is large it may cost £300–£400 to restore. If the problem is in an area where there are many colour changes, a simple toning colour wash will not suffice, and minute changes of colour will have to be made by mixing and touching in with a 000 sable brush, which is even more costly in terms of time and money.

Another problem occurs when the artist has used too much linseed oil, which causes the paint to dry very slowly and become shrivelled. The painting can never be fully restored to its original state and instead has to be retouched. Some experts say that the paint can be heated up and floated back, but the process is rarely successful.

If the picture has not been stored properly, and other pictures have leaned against it, the ground may crack under the pressure. If the canvas is of linen or jute rather than cotton it will be better able to cope with this mistreatment, and stretcher marks should not be visible for quite a while. To remedy the problem, the picture should be lined under pressure. In this respect a compo lining is better than a wax lining.

Oil paintings often suffer from mildew and fungal problems. The problem with black mould is that it goes through the paint rather than resting on the surface. It will also go through the varnish and thus has to be scraped off and retouched. It is time-consuming to touch out small dark marks and results in a lot of expense. For example, a picture by Frank Moss Bennett about 60cm square having black mould and other faults cost almost £1,000 to restore.

The problem of fly marks cannot generally be resolved with the application of chemicals. They have to be scraped off and then touched in. Often someone will paint a frame or touch it up without removing the picture from the frame, leaving marks of gold paint on the picture surface. This may stick to the varnish or may go through to the oil paint. In any case the gold paint has to be scraped off and the picture surface cleaned. Sometimes a glaze of colour has to be applied to disguise the area where the gold paint has been, and this is followed by a re-varnish. Therefore, it is not a simple matter of wiping off the alien gold paint.

One of the essential skills of restoring oil paintings is to be able to remove varnish and layers of paint, which have been added since the picture was painted, without damaging the original paint. Frequently acetone is used, diluted with white spirit. The careful restorer will start with a very dilute mixture and strengthen it as he gains experience working on a particular painting.

Restorers: It is advisable only to use a restorer recommended by a person or an institute who is professionally knowledgeable about restoration, e.g. a reputable gallery owner, an auction house, a museum or a municipal art gallery. Regrettably, a poor, unskilled or inexperienced restorer can damage a picture irreparably. Good restorers are generally very busy, so they may hold a picture for months – possibly many months. This may be something to consider when you buy, if you want to see the picture on the wall immediately or want to sell it quickly. A good county-by-county guide to repairers and restorers of art and antiques is *The Bonhams Directory* (1993), compiled by Tim Forrest and John Kirkwood.

If you are buying from a dealer, you should ask how much restoration has been carried out on the picture you are considering. You can ask to use an ultraviolet lamp. If the dealer says it has just been cleaned with one or two bits of touching up, he won't mind you using the lamp. If 90 per cent has been overpainted, then it may be a picture to avoid. But it also depends on the price which may reflect the amount of restoration and overpainting, e.g. only £1,800 is being asked for a picture that normally would cost £5,000. However, bear in mind that there are some varnishes that render the ultraviolet lamp ineffective.

Cleaning: Having bought a picture in its original condition, do you have it cleaned? This is inadvisable, unless it is essential. If a picture looks too pristine and new, it can reduce the price when selling at auction. Having said that, one notes that pictures in major London galleries look as if they were very recently painted. Many dealers put a light glaze over areas of discoloration and use a very shiny varnish. Presumably this is in the belief that that is what their potential clients – collectors or dealers – are looking for.

Framing

An original frame may communicate a good deal about the picture it surrounds. If it is elaborate and expensive, it is likely to house a valuable picture. A cheap modern frame suggests a cheap, and possibly modern picture. Clearly, if you are framing an old picture in good condition with the intention of selling it, you should look for an old frame contemporary with the painting. To have what appears to be the original frame in good condition on a picture can add a third or more to its price.

Frames for oils are heavier and wider than those used for prints or water-colours. For oils, the canvas should fit well within the frame, with just a little space to allow for movement in the stretcher. Ideally, the picture should be attached to the frame with small copper plates, but a common practice is to put nails into the frame and bend them over the stretchers. It is obvious, but nevertheless sometimes ignored, that the various components of the hanging system should be strong enough. The fixing to the wall, the hanging wire or the cord and the fixing to the frame need to be adequate and not, for example, rusted or frayed.

Frames are easily damaged and are often bumped against doorways, put on the ground whilst the boot of the car is opened or damaged in transit. Within the auction house they are usually treated less well than they deserve, and often one sees pictures piled against one another without any protective padding separating them. Damaged frames can generally be readily restored. Unless the frame is of exceptional value, restoration can be undertaken by the amateur.

Ideally, a painting should be set in a frame which is, in effect, an airtight box, having a sealed glass front and a tight backing. A frame may be worth more than the picture it contains, so that it may be worthwhile to pay a lot for a picture in poor condition if it is in a wonderful frame.

Mounts

A picture on a thin support such as paper needs a suitable mount. It cannot otherwise be handled safely. It is so easy to put a slight kink or crease in a large piece of paper when moving it or turning it over. The mounting board should be of pure rag fibre. Pulp boards cause great damage.

Fakes

Everyone recalls the great forgeries – the Jan Vermeers of Han van Meegeren and the Samuel Palmers of Tom Keating. Both forgers set out to fool the art establishment and succeeded brilliantly, showing that highly respected experts could be wrong. Christopher Wright in his book, *The Art of the Forger*, demonstrates how a number of paintings bought by international museums for millions of dollars are forgeries and are worth very little.

It is useful to recognize that copies are not forgeries. Many artists, both as students and in their mature years, have developed their skill and art by copying the work of great masters. Many of these are of well-known paintings and are unsigned. Currently, there is a flourishing trade in the copying of pictures. For a few hundred pounds one can have what appears to be an original work of art by a famous artist, and one need not tell one's friends. If they were to look on the back they might find that it is marked as a copy indelibly. Clearly, it is not difficult for the unscrupulous to forge a signature on such paintings. Such actions are intentions to deceive and, as such, are criminal. But not all intentions to deceive are so blatant and can escape the rigours of the law. For example, it is not illegal to put a name on a frame or mount to suggest that something is other than it actually is. Many such examples of this occur in the sales rooms.

Other deceptions which are not illegal include putting a

recently painted picture in a genuinely old frame, using old backing materials, old labels or markings on the back of the picture. Less reprehensible, but nevertheless misleading, is the current plethora of seemingly old paintings in simulated old frames, many of which come from the Far East.

There are many unsigned pictures in circulation, and some of these acquire signatures by individuals who specialize in forging them. There are books of signatures and monograms which you can consult to assess whether a signature is genuine. An example is John Castagno's *European Artists: Signatures and Monograms, 1800–1990*. However, keep in mind that the forger is also aware of these books. Where an auction house believes the signature to be genuine, it describes the work as being 'signed'; where they have doubts about the signature, they use the phrase 'bears a signature'.

It is difficult to detect very good fakes. It is less important if you pay a fraction of the price that a genuine original would cost – all that has happened is that you have not made a killing. However, if you pay the right price and you have a fake, then it is serious.

Fakes often seem to be too perfect. Tell-tale signs are whether the varnish has any crackle on the surface, whether the brushstrokes look right or the signature laboured, or whether the signature on an oil painting is in a different colour from any that has been used elsewhere in the painting. If a supposedly old picture shows no signs of wear, this should sound a warning-bell to the buyer.

Sometimes pictures are put in old frames with old board, but careful inspection will show that the edges have recently been cut. Nails can be made to look old, and in any case there are plenty of old nails about.

To avoid fakes, it is helpful to specialize and become familiar with one artist or a few, learning about what kind of canvases they used, what their subject-matter, colours, range and type of brush strokes are like, and what their method of painting was, e.g. working from light to dark or dark to light.

It is important to be able to date a canvas, because there are many copies. For example, a copy of a Stanhope Forbes painting may be signed 'S. Forbes'. To be able to detect this, it is important to look at as many pictures as possible – the back as well as the front of each one, the colours used on the canvas, the weave, the wording on the canvas, such as the manufacturer's name, etc. Some canvases can be dated from the trade marks that appear on the back (see Appendix 2).

Great fakes have generally been detected by the appearance of the picture. For example, an article of clothing or a piece of furniture such as a mirror in what is purported to be a seventeenth-century picture is often found not to be of the correct period but perhaps of the twentieth century. Often the lack of quality in the draughtsmanship or the application of paint has been a give-away as to the correct age.

Many buyers of pictures are mesmerized by a name. With a signature, one can look up the artist in the price books or through the *Art Sales Index* and can get very excited about what seems to be a find. Some artists have been copied relentlessly – an example is Myles Birket Foster – and a fundamental question to ask yourself is whether the picture in front of you is painted with the skill that is appropriate to the artist whose signature appears on the picture.

Summary

Condition, the cost and practicability of restoration, the frame and the genuineness of the picture are all factors to take into consideration when buying, particularly when you are doing it on your own. To a large extent, you are protected when you buy from a good gallery. Otherwise, it is largely a matter of looking at a picture carefully. It is very easy to fail to spot the pale 'burn' marks or indentations, scratches and fading, etc. on works on paper. Take oil paintings off the wall and look at them at an angle with a view to spotting defects or overpainting. Use the check-list referred to in Chapter 6 as a means of learning progressively as you buy. Take a restorer with you to a sale if you are in doubt about condition, but do not necessarily depend on him to give you advice on the commercial side of things. Treat signatures and price book information with caution. Get to know your artists, and make up your own mind whether the picture is genuine or not.

6 Buying at Auction – Before the Sale

The Scene

An auction is a piece of theatre. On view are the results of the work and experience of many talented artists. In the auction room are a number of experienced and knowledgeable dealers, collectors and gallery owners. Above the multitude – in a pulpit or at a table – is the auctioneer who, often but not always, is a highly professional and canny expert on both paintings and human nature.

Each participant at the auction is invited to decide, in a matter of seconds, the price he or she is willing to pay for a particular lot. It is like a horse-race meeting speeded up. Sums of money, often large, are being pledged. Fear and greed oscillate within each human breast. For at least one person, each lot represents an exciting challenge, almost a matter of life and death. Yet all but the occasional member of the general public affect a casual nonchalance. All but the uninitiated are polished actors, on stage, each with his or her own scenario and script. One is smartly dressed and conveys the aura of being an important dealer. Another, in shabby clothes, is acting the part of a dithering old fool but is actually buying for London dealers. Yet another dodges about as if he has no intention of buying, but from time to time can be seen bidding clandestinely behind the crowd that always congregates at the doorway. And then there are the sellers, watching whether their pictures sell at a good price or are knocked down for very little. Many of the trade – the dealers – are both buyers and sellers.

Advantages and Disadvantages of Buying at Auction

Perhaps the main perceived advantage of buying at auction is that you can obtain a picture cheaper than you could at a gallery. Because many pictures sold at auction subsequently appear in galleries, it is evident that they have been marked up to cover restoration and reframing, the various costs incurred between the hammer price and the restored and reframed picture arriving at the gallery and the need of the gallery owner to cover overheads and make a profit. Other advantages are the wide choice available at auction and the opportunity to see some paintings in their original, unrestored state.

The most telling disadvantage is that you are on your own and, if you don't know what you are doing, you may pay too much or buy a faded or damaged picture or a fake. You are competing with experts. You are going out to bat against the equivalent of a highly skilled county eleven.

On the other hand, if you buy from a gallery, the responsibility for the condition and authenticity of the picture is taken from your shoulders. If the picture is not right, you can take it back. If you find you don't like it, you can probably do a deal with the gallery to buy another picture.

In theory, and often in practice, you can take a fake back if you have bought it at auction. It all depends on the auction house rules and the description in the catalogue as will be discussed in the 'Attribution and Fakes' section below. Provided you are aware of the many pitfalls and traps at an auction and know how to avoid them, it is possible to buy well and subsequently sell at a profit.

How to Read the Catalogue

Every auction sale has a catalogue which gives a list of what is for sale. It is numbered and, in many picture auctions, the sequence of numbers, which is the sequence in which the items will be sold, is quite arbitrary. If there are some highly desirable pictures, they may be put at the end of the catalogue to persuade buyers to stay to the last, and presumably be tempted on the way. Generally, prints are separated from water-colours which, in turn, are separated from oils. Catalogues range from photocopied lists all the way to luxuriously illustrated volumes each costing as much as a Dover sole lunch.

Each item is numbered and is described, often with the size of the picture, and any information as to whether it is signed, dated or with any exciting bits of information. Often – but there are many exceptions – there are estimates, generally a range e.g. £400–£500. (For further discussion about catalogue descriptions and estimates see below.)

If you are a regular buyer or you have paid the required subscription, you will be sent a catalogue. If not, you have to buy one. If you can, get a catalogue in advance of viewing as this enables you to spot anything that meets your criteria, examples of which have been discussed in chapter 3. Occasionally this is not possible as the catalogue is only available on the day of the sale. Some auctions hold sales that are non-catalogue sales, and the item is sold by the lot number on the ticket stuck or attached to the picture.

If you want to make money, you have the most difficult task of all, because there will be a number of very astute dealers, runners and gallery owners competing with you. The first question is: 'If you buy it, can you sell it?' If the answer is 'yes', then the next question is: 'Can you buy it at a price that will show you a profit?' To outwit everyone else, you have not only to spot something that answers both questions 'yes', but also something which no one else is likely to want – because, for example, they do not recognize the artist or do not believe the painting is by the artist stated in the catalogue. Needless to say it has to be 'right', not a fake. Naturally, you cannot make up your mind about that from a catalogue. What you can do is mark possibilities, and check them in the biographical and price books. If you know collectors or dealers who might be interested, you might ring them up and see what they are willing to pay you to buy for them. If you are a collector, the catalogue tells you if your particular artist or subject is in the sale. If you want to know what the picture looks like – colour, style, frame and condition – you have to go and view.

Viewing

Viewing days will usually be the two or three days immediately before the sale. It is generally possible to view on the day of the sale – but not always. If the sale starts at 11 a.m., for example, it may be possible to view from 9 a.m. The trade often view on the day of the sale, so it is quite hectic with dealers taking pictures off the wall to look at their backs, and others moving steps around to see pictures high up. One or two of the trade will view as the picture is held up for sale – a piece of one-upmanship. However, ideally you should view as early as you can, as this allows you time to do research, look up the biographical and price books. On the morning of the sale, you can check up on what you might previously have missed or what your research has revealed you should look for.

When you go into the sale room, it is a good idea to have a quick look around to see if anything stands out. Next, you can look for the pictures you have already marked in the catalogue. Finally, you can try to look at everything.

Sometimes this can be done methodically by starting at Lot 1 and going through to the end, provided the auctioneers have displayed the pictures in the same sequence as the catalogue. However, some auction rooms display them to suit themselves in any old sequence, and so it is a tedious process to check off everything in the catalogue. At the end of all this, you probably have to find a porter or assistant to ask where, for example, No. 37 is. Often, the unfindable ones are miniatures, small items and items likely to get damaged or stolen, which are locked in glass-fronted cabinets. There is generally someone standing guard who will let you see them. Folios of water-colours or drawings may be closeted in some corner.

The important things to look for in a particular picture are described below but to assist you in the sale room, a check-list has been included as Appendix 3.

This process of looking is a great deal more difficult than might at first appear. The first general look around requires one to be in a receptive frame of mind, to be open to the impact of the pictures. It is like going into a room full of people – sometimes one or two individuals stand out. It may be their beauty or their character, or they may have a compelling charisma or confidence. It is the same with a roomful of pictures. Some days there will be nothing, but on other days several pictures will make an impact.

The second stage is to look at the pictures you have marked because of the artist, subject, estimate or some other attribute. For each picture, assess whether it makes a favourable impression. Would you like to have it on your wall? Then look at it in detail, using the check-list, particularly assessing the condition and the authenticity. It is not easy to maintain close attention to all the detail. It requires one to avoid being distracted in any way, to be in the 'here and now'. It follows that this is best done alone. Accompanied by a friend or spouse or colleague, it is virtually impossible to give full attention to each picture.

The third stage is to try to look at everything else to see whether you have missed anything. This is difficult and, unless you are very expert, you are in danger of speculating, i.e. taking a chance where the odds may be stacked against you. As succeeding sections of this chapter will demonstrate, there are many traps for the unwary.

The Image: So, to repeat the point, the first thing to do is to ask whether the picture is attractive. Would you like to live with it? Is it well painted? Is there interesting detail? Is there something beyond the paint that the image communicates – just as, with good poetry, there is something more than the words and the meaning. Is there a sort of magic?

Images that are referred to as 'commercial' are those which dealers can sell to the public. They include country scenes with animals or pretty girls. On the whole, images of children or girls are more commercial than those of old people although there are exceptions – for example 'old salts' and the old men in Charles Spencelayh's paintings. Dogs, cats and horses are very popular – in fact most animals and birds have a following. Many images are sought in a particular area – for example, those of colleges in Oxford and Cambridge. Pictures that tell a story, often Victorian and sentimental, have a following. It is important to know and recognize images that are in demand, and these may be discovered by visiting many dealers' galleries.

The Size and Shape: There is a limited market for large pictures. Most people do not live in mansions. A large painting not only needs wall space but you have to be able to get a reasonable distance away from it to view it properly. Further, if it is a very large picture with an equally large frame, carriers might have to be engaged with all the additional expense that this entails.

Very small paintings, including miniatures, represent something of a specialist market.

Most people's homes can accommodate pictures in the

range 15cm–75cm. Most pictures are rectangular, with either the vertical height being greater than the horizontal, which is called 'portrait', or the other way round, 'landscape'. Not surprisingly, portraits are generally best in the 'portrait' shape and landscapes in the 'landscape' shape. Which to buy, all things being more or less equal, might depend on the place on the wall of the house or office that needs filling. There are many other shapes – the square, the circular tondo which is quite popular with some artists (particularly the Victorian painters), the lunette, the semi-circular, the oval, the diptych (two panels) and the triptych (three panels).

Recognizing Condition Problems and How to Assess their Effect on the Intrinsic Value

The possible defects and condition problems have already been discussed in chapter 5 and the check-list in Appendix 3 can assist you in making your examination. Only practice, experience and concentration will enable you to spot these and determine whether repair and rectification is possible at all and, if it is, how much it is going to cost to put it right. Even so, it is better to buy a picture with no defects, providing it is in its original condition. It is important to watch out for, if not to avoid altogether, pictures that have been badly or over-restored. Initially, these can often appear to be in good condition; close inspection is therefore very important.

How to Equate the Aesthetic Appeal with the Commercial Value

'Aesthetic appeal' is the value placed on a painting for its own beauty in accordance with the principles of good taste. 'Commercial value' is the intrinsic value of a picture established by the commercial art world that brings into play a number of considerations to a lesser or greater degree, such as the following factors.

'Equate' in this context means the interrelationship of the aesthetic and intrinsic considerations which affect the price and the advisability of making a purchase. Sometimes these considerations conflict and sometimes they reinforce each other.

Age: how old a painting is, and any value it may have because of its age.

The artist: who painted it, and how highly valued the work of the artist is, whether it be at local, national or international level.

Academic: the scholarly value, in consideration of age, subject-matter, construction, the artist, etc.

Emotional: the sentimental value that may be shared by innumerable people or by only a few, i.e. a painting of a loved one may only have value for you or your immediate family unless the loved one happens also to be an internationally famous film star.

The Frame

The condition and quality of the frame may be significant. If it is undamaged or only slightly damaged, the frame may be worth more than the picture in it. Sometimes a painting painted last year in Hong Kong is put into an old damaged frame to persuade you that the painting is Victorian. Many water-colours, at auction, are in brand new frames with elaborate mounts. The plus side of this is that a gallery or private purchaser can immediately put them on the wall, but it does indicate that they have been done up for the sale – not necessarily a bad thing but something to bear in mind.

Attribution and Fakes

Although most people would claim to know what is meant by fake, this is not a term favoured by the trade, because there are often good reasons why it is inappropriate. The convention as to the integrity of attribution (in other words, whether the picture is by the artist stated) is that if the work is catalogued with the name(s) or recognized designation of the artist, it is, in the auctioneer's opinion, a work by the artist. The practical effect of this is that if a painting so designated subsequently turns out to be not by the artist, you can take it back to the auction house and get your money back. There are provisos – there is generally a time limit stated, within which the auctioneer has to be informed in writing that the item is a forgery, the item has to be returned in the same condition as when it was bought, and the buyer has to produce evidence, for example, an expert opinion, that the item is a forgery. The time limit varies from auctioneer to auctioneer from a week or two to several years, and the conditions also vary. It is important to read the small print in every catalogue, or, if it is not in the catalogue, the conditions of sale – which will be available somewhere in the auction rooms.

If the forenames of the artist, or initials with following asterisks and the surname, are not given, then this is an indication that the auction house does not have the firm opinion that the painting is the work of that particular artist. There are a series of phrases to indicate a scale of increasing uncertainty. 'Attributed to' means that it is probably the work of the artist. One of the ways in which money can be made is to buy an 'attributed' picture, which one is pretty certain is really by the artist. However, the probability implied by the word 'attributed' varies considerably from 'there is a chance that it might be by the artist' to 'it almost certainly is, but we can't be sure.' There are a great many forgeries about and, unless you are very sure, it is best to regard 'attributed to' as 'not likely to be' the artist, whose signature appears on the picture.

'Circle of' means work of the same period as the artist and possibly executed under the influence of the 'circle' of which the artist was a member. The circle can be very big. 'Follower of' means work of the same period of the artist but not by the artist. 'Manner of' means work in the style of the artist but of a later date. 'After' means a copy of any date of the work of the artist.

Whether a painting is 'right', i.e. whether the signature or monogram has been put on the canvas or paper etc. by the artist, is frequently the subject of knowing looks by the trade, i.e. the dealers, runners, gallery retailers; and possibly by some collectors. The matter is somewhat complicated by the fact that some artists, in the past, have signed their work with someone else's name. There are a not inconsiderable number of paintings which are sold at auction without signature, which subsequently acquire them. This is clearly fraud and should not happen, but it has been happening down the ages. The doubts of the trade will arise from their knowledge of subject-matter, the technique used to paint the picture, the age of the paper or canvas, the condition of the paint and the colours used, and the signature itself. Viewing the picture with the aid of an ultraviolet lamp may disclose additions to the painting of a later date including a signature. With old water-colours, it will be reassuring if the painting has never been taken out of its frame. However, this can be faked too.

A convention used by some auction houses is to use the term 'signed and/or dated and/or inscribed', for works that are from the hand of the artist, in the auctioneer's opinion – which, remember, is not to be taken as a statement of fact. The term 'bears a signature and/or date and/or inscription' mean that, in the auctioneer's opinion, they have been added by another hand.

Some assistance can be gained by consulting the books of signatures and monograms referred to in chapter 5. Such books can enable you to identify a picture which the auctioneer has missed or which he has indicated the signature to be illegible – 'indistinctly signed'. However, forgers also have access to such books and may be clever enough to make the signature indistinct but just discernible.

The process of viewing is often an oscillation between looking at the catalogue and looking at the picture, which can be trying on the eyes. If you are interested in certain artists, some catalogues assist you by having an index of artists in alphabetical order at the back. After a while, you will have homed in on pictures you are interested in. If all seems well, concentrate on the price.

Provenance

It is sometimes possible to discover where a painting came from. Has it come from the private home of a well-known collector, or has it been put in the sale by a runner or dealer, who has been unable to sell it elsewhere? Provenance is highly important for Old Master paintings or very expensive pictures. Much museum research is concerned with establishing the history of a painting: who owned it, where it has been exhibited, what sales it has been in. Sometimes the catalogue will give details of provenance. Sometimes it will be possible to gain some clues from the back of the painting.

Many important collectors in the past have marked their drawings by hand or with a stamp – usually at the edge or the reverse. Fritz Lugit has recorded many marks and provided information about the owners of prints and drawings in Les Marques de collections de dessins et d'estampes (Amsterdam, 1921, suppl. The Hague, 1956).

Exhibition and Gallery Labels

Most galleries put a stock/exhibition label on the back of the picture or the frame. Some labels contain minimal information – artist's name, title of picture, and price. Other galleries – for example, Frost & Reed, Stacey Marks and Newlyn Orion – quote additionally their stock/archive number, the date, medium, size and exhibition details, together with a note on the label advising the purchaser not to remove the label as these have proved invaluable for the purposes of authentication and provenance. Agnew's stock labels can be checked back for over a hundred years. Christie's have used a system of numbers and letters, which may often be found on framed pictures that have passed through their hands. Framemakers labels can also be found.

From all these sources, enquiries can be made and often useful information obtained in the search for provenance or identity.

Estimates

Many, but by no means all, catalogues give estimates for each lot – generally a lower and a higher figure, which suggests a range within which the auctioneer expects the picture to sell. Some auctioneers give estimates for pictures over a certain amount (often £100, sometimes £200) with the implication that if there is no estimate against an item in the catalogue, the auctioneer's estimate is less than £100 (or £200) – but also with the possible implication that the auctioneer doesn't know what the picture is worth.

Next, you wonder if the estimate is realistic. Sometimes the auctioneer will put a low estimate on a picture to attract buyers to the sale in the expectation of getting a bargain. Sometimes the seller has insisted on an unrealistically high price. You have recourse to the price books or the data bank services such as the *Art Sales Index*. You may find no entries, one or two entries or a lot of entries. If no entries, you have to fall back on the bibliography books to assess whether the artist is significant. If there are a few entries, do not confuse water-colours with oils. Also remember that the price books generally have a lower limit below which they will not make an entry. For example, many of your artist's pictures may have sold at a number of auctions for say

£100–150, which you would not know, but a few may have exceeded £500 and these will be the ones listed. If there are many entries, you will be surprised to see the range of prices – maybe from £600 to £35,000. Often there does not seem to be a good reason for this price variation – larger pictures tend to fetch higher prices than small ones, although very large pictures do not. You can generally see at which auction a particular price was obtained. A price obtained at an auction house in Rome is not necessarily a useful guide to the price a similar picture might fetch at auction in Penzance.

Nicholas Houlgate – who describes himself as 'someone who sets some 15,000 estimates every year' – stated in a letter to the *Antique Dealer's Gazette*: 'high estimates indicate to the trade that it is either a trade lot/highly reserved/ unbuyable. A low estimate indicates: a private lot/ unreserved/ignorant auctioneer/bargain'. Peter Lawson-Smith, who describes himself as a 'keen collector of antiques for many years', compared estimates with the prices actually achieved, from a particular issue of the *Antique Trade Gazette*. Errors (price realized minus price estimated divided by price estimated) varied from 32 per cent to 260 per cent. Such discrepancies make news and whilst the vast majority of prices realized fall within the estimates, key lots are under-estimated fairly frequently.

Reserves

The reserve is the least amount of money that the auctioneer's client has authorized him to sell the picture for. This is often a matter of negotation, because the seller wants to get the highest possible price whilst the auctioneer wants a price at which he feels confident the picture will sell.

One auction house identifies four types of reserve:

Fixed reserve: the auctioneer will not sell the item for less than the reserve.

Discretionary reserve: the auctioneer will sell within 10% of the reserve.

Auctioneer's reserve: the auctioneer gets the best price – normally within 20 per cent of the lower estimate.

No reserve: the auctioneer sells for whatever price he can get.

Many auction houses consider that there is no reserve unless instructions to the contrary are given and that these instructions should be in writing. Most auctioneers have a statement in small print to the effect that the auctioneer has discretion to sell at a price 10 per cent below the agreed reserve. Some auctioneers reserve the right to sell below this 10 per cent discretion level, but if they do so, they agree that the seller is entitled to the 10 per cent discretion level. The lower figure in the estimate range may be the reserve, but not necessarily so; it may be much higher or lower, or there may not be a reserve at all.

Buyers do not know what the reserve is, but often guess – sometimes correctly – that it is 10 per cent less than the bottom estimate. However, sometimes the reserve can be higher than the bottom estimate and occasionally, but improperly and misleadingly, above the top estimate.

Commission Bids

If you cannot attend the sale, you can still leave a bid, known as a commission bid. You can get a form from the auctioneer's office on which you can make your bid. On this you provide details about yourself – your name, address, telephone number and bank details – and then you write down the auction reference number or title and date and then the lot number and the money value of the bid you are prepared to make. If there is a reserve, your bid will have to be at or above that figure. You may guess, or even find out, that the auctioneer has discretion to sell at 10 per cent below the reserve. The reserve may be the lower of the two figures in the catalogue but not necessarily so.

If you want to be sure of buying the picture, you will pitch the commission bid high. This does not mean that you will necessarily have to pay that amount. On the day of the sale, the auctioneer may have other commission bids and also bids from the floor, i.e. from people in the auction room or on the telephone. If you have put in a commission bid of £500 and the highest of all the other bids is £400, then you should get the picture for the next bid, which will be your bid and will probably be £420. This is how it works with reputable auction houses, but some less scrupulous ones will run the lot up or bid 'against the wall' up to the commission bid, i.e. to £500 in the example given above.

If you see something that has a low estimate or none at all but which you recognize as being worth a good deal, you may have a difficult decision to make if you are going to leave a commission bid. Perhaps you think it may be worth £2,000. Do you leave a low but generous bid such as £200 or do you leave a bid of £2,000? You may argue that if you bid £2,000 and it goes for £150, that is all you will pay. However, your high bid might alert the auctioneer to the fact that he has missed something, with the result that he takes another look and revises the estimate, thus alerting everyone else. On the other hand, if you leave a £200 bid, someone else may also have spotted the 'snip', attend the auction and get it for £220.

When leaving a commission bid, many dealers use the phrase 'plus one'. This means that they are prepared to pay for one more bid above the figure they would like to pay. This is because many people think in terms of round numbers, and the winning bid is often one bid above a round number. Thus, if you think of leaving a commission bid of, say £300, you may be well advised to put £320 on the form.

You may leave a commission bid even if you are going to attend the sale. You might do this to conceal from others the fact that you are bidding. It also gives you the option to enter the bidding if it goes above your commission bid.

Telephone Bids

Most auction houses are willing to accept telephone bids. Provided you give reasonable notice, the auction house will telephone you as the lot you wish to bid for approaches. There is generally a limited number of telephone lines open, so an early reservation is recommended. The larger auction houses put a lower limit on the value of the lot that you can bid for by telephone – for example, £2,000 – but most provincial houses will accept telephone bids for much less. Do not discuss what you are prepared to pay but say that you will listen to the bidding and ask to be advised when the bidding stops. That is the point at which you should enter the bidding. As far as those actually in the room are concerned, the bid you give may be seen as your first bid. Psychologically, this may put off the other bidders, even though in actuality it might be that you are prepared to go no higher.

If, after viewing, you are undecided whether or not to attend the sale and therefore have not left a written bid, you can telephone commission bids through to the auction house, generally no later than thirty minutes before the start of the sale. A bid by telephone or fax is generally only accepted at the sender's risk.

Summary

There are a number of important activities to be undertaken before the day of the sale: getting and studying the catalogue, undertaking research, viewing with eyes open, checking the price and biographical books again, and listing the things you need to look at on the day of the sale provided the opportunity presents itself. Look at the estimates and decide the maximum you are prepared to pay for the lots you are interested in. Decide whether you want to leave commission bids even though you might attend the sale.

7 Buying at Auction – The Sale

Preparation and Preliminaries

User-friendliness is beginning to permeate the auction rooms. Most auction houses outside London have encouraged local housewives or caterers to provide tea, coffee, cakes and sandwiches – and, sometimes, something more sustaining such as quiches or bacon butties. One auctioneer makes available a collection of reference books so that people can check prices and see whether they have spotted something the others might have missed.

Often there are not enough seats, but this is less of a problem than it might seem as many people like to stand or move around. Sometimes the pictures share a room with furniture. Each sale is different, people will be viewing furniture whilst the picture auction is in progress or vice versa. At one auction house, the volume of pictures to be sold is sometimes so great that during the later stages of the sale, two auctions are held in adjacent rooms at the same time.

Be sure you know when the sale is due to start. If the first lot you are interested in is later on in the sale, you can calculate the time your lot will come up, if you know the rate at which the auctioneer sells. For example, if you are interested in Lot No. 250 and the auctioneer sells at a hundred lots per hour, you can estimate that your lot will come up 2½ hours after the start. Some auctioneers are faster than this, and so it is as well to find out from the auctioneer's office what the rate is likely to be for your particular sale. Also check that the numbering is consecutive and that there are not some big gaps in the numbers – for example, water-colours may finish at Lot No. 125 and oils begin at Lot No. 200.

If you are not known to the auction house, you will need to find out how they expect you to pay. In any event, you will have to register and many auction houses now issue you with a paddle – something like a ping-pong bat with a number on it. Some houses are surprisingly trusting for relatively small amounts and accept cheques, even if they have never seen you before. Others require that your bank is contacted before purchases are released. Cash is always acceptable. The acceptance of credit cards is beginning to take place, but the charge made by the credit card companies is generally passed on to the buyer. Where cards are accepted, commission bidders can settle in this way, but there is generally a limit, for example £2,000. It is a condition of the credit card companies that no purchase settled in this way can be released until seven working days from the date of payment. This condition may be waived by the auction house, but it is as well to find out in advance if they are willing to do so.

It is generally possible to pay as the sale proceeds. Most auction houses have computer systems. It is a bore, if you buy a lot early in the sale and this is all you want, to have to wait hours to collect. Sometimes a friendly porter will get something off the wall for you and let you escape. Other auction houses will not allow pictures to be collected until after the end of the sale. It is best to collect your purchases as soon as possible because the longer a picture stays in most auction houses, the more probable it is that it will get damaged.

The Sale Itself

There is a variety of ways in which the pictures are

presented. In some auction houses, the pictures are removed from the walls and the porters show each picture as its lot number comes up. In others, the pictures are left on the walls and a porter points to the relevant one for each lot number. It is seldom that there is confusion about what is being sold, but it is important for you not only to be aware of the lot number, name of artist, subject, etc., but also to know exactly where the picture is.

You have viewed the painting you want to buy, marked it in the catalogue, and wait with increasing expectation, for the auctioneer to reach your number. As the sale proceeds, you can check the actual prices achieved against the estimates to form some idea as to whether things are going cheaply or the opposite.

You will see the auctioneer taking bids from the floor, but he keeps looking down at his desk. This may be because he has one or more commission bids and he is, in effect, bidding on behalf of those who placed the commission bids. It may be, however, that there is only one person actually bidding although it looks as though there are two persons engaged. The auctioneer is bidding on behalf of the vendor and is trying to get the one bidder to bid up to the reserve. If his bid reaches the reserve, the auctioneer stops bidding on behalf of the vendor, and knocks the item down to the bidder from the floor. It would be wrong for the auctioneer to bid on behalf of the vendor if there were no reserve or to continue to bid on behalf of the vendor beyond the reserve level. This latter practice is often referred to as 'bidding off the wall' and does not take place in reputable auction houses.

If the auctioneer fails to achieve bids up to the reserve price – however this is agreed with the vendor – he may pretend that the picture has sold and call out one of several numbers set aside for unsold pictures, or he may say nothing. Usually, he is not anxious to advertise the fact that pictures are not selling, since this may affect the sentiment of the sale. Nevertheless, some auctioneers do say something like, 'Sorry, I can't let it go for that. Come and see me afterwards.'

When a lot does not sell, it is said to be unsold or 'bought in'. At most sales, a number of lots will be bought in. The percentage of lots unsold is given for many of the sales reported in the *Antiques Trade Gazette*, both as a percentage of lots and a percentage in money. The percentage can be as high as 75 per cent but is more usually 20–30 per cent. This will surprise you if you have not attended many auctions, because to the uninitiated everything seems to have sold.

You may have failed to secure something you wanted and be under the misapprehension that someone else bought it. It may, however, have been bought in. It is worthwhile, therefore, to check before you leave the auction rooms. If it was bought in, the auctioneers may, then and there, be able to get in touch with the seller to see if he is willing to accept what you are prepared to offer. He may accept or counter with a higher price and you may be prepared to negotiate. Failing this, you can leave an offer.

If the auctioneer has more than one commission bid, he will probably open the bidding by saying 'I am bid x pounds' and will then call out the lower of the commission bids. You have to be careful when you are a bidder from the floor intent on buying and the auctioneer is bidding commissions, to be sure at the end of the bidding that the picture has been knocked down to you. All too often, someone will think they have secured an item, when the auctioneer has actually knocked it down to the commission bidder. Before he does this he should say something like 'it is now against you all'. If he does not do this, it is probably just an oversight, but there is always a suspicion that the auctioneer is favouring the commission buyer. You can, in theory, check before the hammer goes down, by calling out, 'Is the bid with me?' But if it is all done very quickly, you can only make a fuss immediately afterwards. The auctioneer can then put the item up again or decline to do so – there is no right of appeal.

The actual process of bidding is simple. You wave your hand, the auction catalogue or paddle and shout out if the auctioneer doesn't see you. Generally, he does and once he sees you are bidding, you can give a slight nod of your head or movement of your hand. Some people go to considerable lengths to conceal the fact that they are bidding. If you go to the front of the room and look back, it is often difficult to see who, if anyone, is bidding. Dealers are concerned that if someone sees them bidding, it may indicate that they are on to a good thing and that this may encourage others to enter the fray and put the price up. If you wish to bid anonymously, you can always place a commission bid.

You should decide before the bidding starts whether you are going to get the lot at all costs or whether you are going to go to a particular price and no further. Your decision depends on many things – for example, whether the picture is of sentimental or emotional value to you or one of your loved ones; whether you think you have spotted something worth a lot of money that the others haven't spotted; or whether you are only looking for bargains. The key point is to give it a lot of thought beforehand. Many mistakes are made by lack of clarity of thinking and by not sticking to the discipline of 'I'll pay that much and no more'. Many others are made by seeing the bidding process as a fight between you and someone else. 'I'll not let him beat me. Who does he think he is!' Bidding at auction is an emotional business, the adrenalin flows freely. It is easy to get carried away.

When you have decided that a lot has arrived which you want to bid for, it is best to wait to see what happens. The bidding may go above what you are prepared to pay, in which event you keep your counsel, and think about the next lot you are interested in. If however it doesn't and the bidding begins to falter, this is the time to make a bid in a confident manner. Do not hesitate too long or the hammer may go down. The auctioneer when accepting your bid may say 'new bidder'. This may discourage the previous bidder, the under-bidder, and the lot may be knocked down to you. However, the under-bidder may bid again, and bidding may proceed between you and him until one or other of you reach your limit. When you enter the bidding you should try to do so at a price which will ensure that your final bid is your upper limit. If your final limit is £320, you should enter the bidding say at £220, if the sequence of bidding is You – £220; Mr X – £250; You – £280; Mr X – £300; You – £320.

To do this you need to know the steps by which the bidding proceeds. This will become evident as the sale goes on. At the low end, the bidding may proceed by £5 intervals. Once the bidding has reached £50, the intervals may become £10. By £200, the intervals may oscillate between £20 and £30 e.g. £220, £250, £280, £300. After £500, the intervals may become £50 and after £1,000, the intervals may become £100 and so on. When the bidding has almost run its course, the auctioneer may allow a bid only a percentage or two above the previous one.

If you suspect that you are the only one bidding, it may be best not to go on but to allow the picture to be 'bought in' and to enquire after the sale, or even behind the scenes whilst it is going on, what the seller will take for it, i.e. is he willing to go below his reserve.

When the bidding for a particular lot stops or seems to stop, the auctioneer will attempt to get more bids. He may comment that the lot is going very cheaply and look at you enquiringly. You may think he is paying you the compliment of knowing a good thing when you see it and you may make a bid. He will then turn to the bidder previous to you as if to say, 'You're not going to let him beat you, are you?' In this way he may push the bidding higher. When there is another halt, he may hesitate and then say something like 'I am selling this now, make no mistake'. He may then spin things out further by saying 'This is your last chance' and may look at the under-bidder. Finally he may say slowly 'Going, going, gone' and bring down the hammer. This procedure is more often seen at major auctions for important items, the idea being to pressurize the under-bidder to make a further bid. At lesser auctions where there may be 1,000 lots to sell in a day, the procedure is far more streamlined.

Sleepers

A sleeper is a picture sold at auction, the true identity and value of which is unrecognized, except by the buyer. Everyone is on the look-out for sleepers. If you think you have found one, you will not need much encouragement to keep it to yourself. Clearly, it is a great opportunity to make a lot of money. From the seller's point of view, it represents a big loss and it may be an occasion for litigation against the auctioneer.

That sleepers exist is due to the large numbers of pictures that pass through auction houses, so that one or two items get missed. Some auction houses which are offshoots of major houses have potential sleepers from time to time, some of which are withdrawn by the day of the sale. Evidently someone has come down from Mount Olympus and has spotted the potential sleepers! In spite of this, sleepers tend to turn up most frequently in the busier auction houses, but the possibility of discovering one or two exists at any auction sale. Beware of the unscrupulous dealer who is ready to exploit the inexperienced searcher for sleepers by purposely making some worthless picture look as though it may be the find of a lifetime – for example, by covering it with dirt and varnish.

The phrase 'Attributed to', as well as less enthusiastic attributions, may sometimes be indicators of a potential sleeper.

Discovering sleepers by removing overpaint is an expensive gamble which might turn out to be a loss, because the cost of restoration can be very high, and there may only be rubbish underneath. Also, if the overpaint is of similar age to the original, it is very difficult to remove without removing the paint underneath. Sometimes, a disastrous cleaning has removed much of the painting, and the overpainting has been done to conceal this.

One of the most famous sleepers, discovered by a well known and highly experienced runner, was a painting of *Pope Clement VII* by the sixteenth-century Italian painter Sebastiano del Piombo. The runner bought it for £180, and it was subsequently sold at another auction house for £380,000. Reportedly, the Getty Foundation subsequently paid £6,500,000 for it. We are indebted to Philip Mould for this example taken from his absorbing book *Sleepers: In Search of Lost Old Masters*, which vividly recounts a number of real-life stories of discovering sleepers.

Buyers' Premium

Most auction houses manage to achieve something which is the envy of many other businesses. They get a commission from both the seller and the buyer. It used, not long ago, to be otherwise, when only the seller paid. Then it was clear that the auctioneer was acting for the seller, as an estate agent does. Today most auction houses charge the buyers a premium, often as much as, if not more than, the sellers'.

The buyer's premium has climbed in recent years so that many of the major auction houses now charge 15 per cent on the first £30,000 and 10 per cent on the remaining amount. Elsewhere 10 per cent is the norm, but there are still some auction houses where no premium is charged.

Value Added Tax (VAT)

Normally, at auction, the only VAT paid on the hammer price for most pictures is that applied to the buyer's premium, so that 15 per cent and 10 per cent become 17.625 per cent and 11.75 per cent. Thus a £500 hammer price costs you £588 for 15 per cent premium and £559 for 10 per cent premium. It is clearly important to take this into account when deciding how much you are prepared to bid.

However, there are some lots, generally marked in the catalogue with a dagger or in some other way, which attract VAT on the hammer price as well as on the buyer's premium. These might be, for example, pictures put into auction by an hotel. The dagger is very easy to miss in the excitement. Thus such a picture, with a hammer price of £500 would attract VAT of £87.50, which added to the £588 above comes to £675.50 – quite a nasty surprise if you were not expecting it.

New VAT regulations mean that the buyer's premium percentage should be inclusive of VAT. Thus one auction house has interpreted the new VAT regulations to charge 14.68 per cent on the first £30,000 (12.5 per cent plus 17.5 per cent VAT) and 11.75 per cent on the excess over £30,000 (10 per cent plus 17.5 per cent VAT). Note that 15 per cent becomes 17.625 per cent under the new regulations.

Withdrawals, Revised Descriptions, Estimates and Extra Lots

One of the most exasperating occurrences at auctions is the withdrawal of lots. You have viewed and spotted some lots that the auctioneers seem to have undervalued substantially. You have done your homework, looked them up in the books and turn up on the day, eager for the auction to start. Suddenly, someone bustles into the sale room and posts up a notice. This is a list of withdrawals, and the law of cussedness will frequently dictate that they include your 'snips'. Clearly the auction house has initially failed to recognize the value of the lot. Subsequently, the vendor may have become aware that his very valuable picture was in the company of very minor works.

Equally irritating is the revised description, which, again, is usually the auctioneer's mistake in initial valuation. It may arise from a work that was attributed to the artist becoming the genuine article in the view of the auction house – or vice versa. If you had known it was genuine, you would have attended the sale in the hope that no one else knew so that you could get it at an 'attributed' price. The downgrading of a lot can be equally frustrating if one has turned up to buy 'a work by the artist'.

This change in the catalogue terminology as to attribution will clearly cause a change in the estimate, but, even if this is not so, not infrequently the estimate will be revised, usually substantially upwards. If one has travelled a long distance for the sale, these revisions may result in a wasted day and considerable cost.

Less disrputive is the introduction of extra lots, but beware of these as you will not have had the opportunity of a careful scrutiny.

The Small Print

The rules and regulations and the conditions of sale are set out to a greater or lesser degree in the catalogue. Sometimes, they are posted on the wall of the sale room or below the auctioneer's pulpit. It is as well to be aware of them.

Most auction houses make it clear in their conditions of sale that they act as agents only and take no responsibility for any faults or defects or the correctness of any statements as to almost anything. Everything they say are statements of opinion, not to be relied upon. Once the hammer has fallen, the purchaser is totally responsible. Generally, the auctioneers have absolute discretion to settle any dispute.

Some auctioneers do not allow lots to be removed whilst the sale is in progress. Others do, provided they have been paid for. This is helpful, if one only wants one or two early lots. Otherwise, you have to hang about or go off and come back to pick up your purchases. It is useful to find out what the rules are.

There is generally a limit of time within which the lots bought must be paid for, and removed from the auction premises. Some auction houses say 'immediately after the conclusion of the sale', otherwise they will not hold themselves responsible for loss, damage, etc. Some exact penalties if the lots are not paid for within a short period – say, two days. Others are more accommodating, for example, giving seven days to pay and twenty-eight days to remove. After the stipulated time has elapsed, storage charges are usually payable, and you may find, especially in London, that your lots have been whisked off to some remote warehouse, incurring both high transportation costs and storage charges.

Non-payment or failure to collect according to the auction house rules may attract a variety of remedies ranging from proceedings against the buyer, storage and insurance charges, interest on the purchase price, or even reselling the lot(s) without reserve(s), and the buyer still being responsible for any shortfall plus the additional costs incurred by the auctioneer having to reoffer the lot(s).

Get to Know Your Auctioneer

Auctioneers come in all shapes and sizes. It has been said that an auctioneer has to be a combination of psychologist, actor, artist and mathematician. It is a highly skilled profession. The auctioneer has to have confidence and conviction, be aware of what is happening on the floor, check that the goods being offered match the description in the catalogue, get a momentum of bidding going, have regard to commission bids and reserves, and get the correct name or paddle number and the correct amount for each bid. Generally, the auctioneer has a clerk sitting beside him or her, who enters the price and bidder's details on a form. Periodically, this form is taken to the accounts office, the information from which is used to draw up an invoice for each bidder, either by hand or by a computer.

Often there is a sort of parent-child relationship between the auctioneer in his pulpit and the buyers on the floor, which can intimidate the inexperienced buyer. Traditionally, many dealers address the auctioneer as 'Sir'. Some auctioneers hustle and put the bidder under considerable pressure. One or two keep on repeating the price as if they were at a Texas cattle market. Some are genial and understanding like a kind headmaster, others have a harsh approach, reminiscent of a drill sergeant, yet others appear academic and possibly a little flustered. They are all trying to make sure the lots are sold, and they are all trying to push the price up.

Because the auctioneer takes a fee from both the seller and the buyer, he has to appear to favour neither. Clearly, the buyer likes to think that he can get a bargain at a particular auction house, whilst the seller likes to think that the auctioneer can achieve very good prices. If one is both a buyer and a seller, one hopes to buy and sell well but it is probably inadvisable to sell your pictures at an auction where you repeatedly get bargains.

The auctioneer is often closely concerned with cataloguing the pictures and will generally have been involved in deciding the authenticity of the pictures and the estimates. It is therefore a good idea to make friends and seek his advice. It may be necessary to make an appointment to do this on one of the viewing days. It is unlikely that he will be able to see you on the day of the sale.

Who is at the Sale?

Auctions attract a wide variety of people. There are the private purchasers – collectors or just those who want to buy the odd picture or two. There are those who own galleries, buying pictures to hang on their walls or to restore and reframe. There are those buying on behalf of collectors or galleries. Then there are the entrepreneurs who buy speculatively to sell on to galleries and collectors or to put pictures back into other auctions. These are variously referred to as 'the trade' or as 'runners'.

It is an interesting and, in many ways, a wonderful community, sharing the comradeship of being at risk and 'putting one's money where one's mouth is'. Around the walls, at a typical sale, are the fruits of many skilled, intelligent and creative men and women. In the auction room are experts, highly experienced traders and specialists, some looking like businessmen, some like weekenders in pullovers and open-necked shirts, some looking as scruffy as Steptoe and Son. But do not be deceived. In the art market, things are seldom what they seem. Against this background, a tremendous piece of theatre is being played out with real people and real money in real time.

Rings and Other Goings-on

Often, dealers or runners find themselves turning up at the same auctions in a particular geographical area. It is inevitable that views and information are exchanged including questions like 'What are you after today?' If there is a feeling of trust between two potential bidders, it is possible that it will be established which of the lots both parties are interested in. Further discussion can lead to each one telling the other how high he is prepared to bid for a particular lot. Properly, each party should bid his own corner, but from time to time one of several possibilities materialize, each moving towards what legally might be regarded as 'hardly playing the game'.

The simplest arrangement is for the two parties – say, Joe Bloggs and A.N. Other – to agree to divide up the lots they both want. So that Joe will not bid for Lot No. 67 whilst

A.N. will keep clear of Lot No. 245. It might get more complicated, with each agreeing not to bid for several lots.

However, say Joe Bloggs is prepared to go to £300, whilst A.N. Other is ready to go to £350. A.N. may say, 'I'll not bid against you unless it goes over £300, and presumably, Joe, you agree the same arrangement on this other lot where I am prepared to go higher than you.' Again, A.N. Other may be a dealer who has sold pictures to Joe Bloggs and hopes to do so again, in which event he will probably say, 'OK, I'll not bid on that lot unless you drop out', which is not very different in effect from the previous proposal. It does however lack precision and, in the heat of the bidding and with only nods and winks going on, it is easy to end up with neither party making the winning bid.

Where several dealers, in this frame of mind, find themselves frequently attending the same auctions and pushing each other's prices up, they may form what is called a ring. (Technically, even the above 'gentlemen's agreements' constitute rings.) This arrangement is illegal and could get the participants into serious trouble if they were found out. What happens is that the ring nominate one of their number to bid whilst the others keep out of it. They may nominate different members of the group for different lots, to allay any suspicions.

The ring agree in advance which lots they are going for and what prices they are willing to go to. After the sale, they will hold an auction amongst themselves, in some discreet location. Alternatively, they may hold their own auction before the sale, which has the advantage that the price one of their number is going to bid up to at the sale is also decided. Occasionally, if suspicions are aroused, the police will catch the post-sale auction going on. The ring is bust and the members chastened and probably prosecuted.

The ring, or even a group of local dealers not operating a ring, can be very defensive if another dealer appears on their patch – that is, starts to bid in the auction houses they regard as their territory. Each time the intruder starts to bid, one of the local group will join in the bidding and push the price beyond what the intruder is hoping to pay, who either finishes up paying too much or fails to secure the lot. Either way, the locals hope the interloper will conclude that the particular auction house is not a good place at which to buy pictures and will keep away This scheme can also be used to dissuade the private buyer from thinking he can get bargains at auction.

The defence against these tactics is not to go beyond the price you have determined before the sale, to lurk behind a pillar or at the doorway of the auction room, so that the local dealers do not know who is bidding, or to remain anonymous by making commission bids.

Summary

Buying at auction is a real-time event, from the moment you enter the sale auction room to the time you pack your successful bids in your car and drive away. It is not easy to stay calm and go methodically through the various communication processes that are essential to have a successful day.

Much of the communication will be with yourself, and this needs to be constructive and on the ball. It is difficult, if you are unfamiliar with auctions, to avoid being self-conscious and to wonder what people are thinking of you. It is best to be on your own. Otherwise, you will be unable to concentrate and, once the sale begins, you may well find that you have missed bidding for a lot you wanted because someone was engaging your attention.

Arrive early, so that parking your car is not a problem. Decide on the best place to stand or sit. Register and be sure of the bidding arrangements. Do they use paddles or cards or do you just call out your name? Make arrangements about paying. Have a good look at the pictures you have researched. With each one, imagine you have bought it and paid the price you have decided upon plus the premium and VAT. So often, after one has bought, one wonders why on earth one has done so, especially as it seemed such a matter of life or death whilst you were bidding.

Use the checklist (Appendix 3). Don't bid too soon or too eagerly. Place commission bids, if you think there is a ring which will bid you up. Don't go beyond the price you have decided upon – at least, not far beyond.

8 Selling at Auction

Reasons for Selling

There are several possibilities which can affect the way you sell at auction. You may wish to sell one or more pictures because you have become tired of them and need a change – there is no urgency and, although money is always important, you are not too fussed about the financial outcome. Or you may need some money fairly quickly. Or you deal in pictures and, having bought some, you want to sell them at the best possible price.

Who are you Selling to?

There are several types of potential customers for the pictures you put into auction.

Private individuals and collectors are generally looking for particular artists or subjects. Price is not too important to them nor, within limits, the condition of the painting, although they may often be attracted by something they can take home and immediately hang on the wall.

Gallery owners are looking for pictures they think they can sell to their customers. If times are good they may be short of stock and want things they can get on to their gallery walls as soon as possible. In more difficult times, they are looking for bargains. Generally, they have clients who are looking for particular artists and/or subjects. Otherwise, they seek popular subjects – dogs, cats, farm animals, hunting scenes, country cottages and haymaking, pretty girls and combinations of these.

Dealers and runners are, for the most part, buying for or on behalf of galleries or collectors. They are generally looking for bargains, but the cost of attending an auction sale is not negligible and so they cannot be influenced entirely by price. What they need is turnover, and to achieve this they often have to put up with small margins and pay the going rate.

Preparing the Pictures for Sale

The phrases that appear time and time again in the *Antiques Trade Gazette* recommending a picture to trade buyers are 'fresh to the market' and 'in unrestored condition'. What the trade is looking for are genuine paintings, hopefully in their original frames, from a private source, which have not been restored. However, the private buyers, and sometimes the galleries, often want pictures that are clean and in nice frames.

Faced with a collection of paintings you wish to sell, you have to decide which market you are going for – the trade, the private owners or the galleries.

If it is the trade, you do not bother to restore or reframe your pictures – don't even clean the glass if it is glazed. If you have an old painting in a relatively new frame, it may be worthwhile to reframe it in an old frame. Such frames turn up at auction or can be bought from frame dealers. If you are aiming for the private buyer, presentation is important. The painting should be clean and in good condition, in a nice frame which has not been damaged. Pictures can be sold unframed if they are oils; or in portfolios if they are water-colours, but it is generally more advantageous to sell them framed.

Choosing the Auction House

The primary consideration is to choose the auction house that will get you the best price – easier said than done. To do this, you take the picture to several houses and ask their opinion as to price and saleability. The opinions you get depend less on the standing of the auction house than on the experience of the person you consult. This is discussed in more detail below under the section 'Reserves and Estimates'.

Further topics to be considered are the charges – the selling commission, the cost of insurance, the cost of illustrations and the buying-in charges if the picture does not sell. Again, these are discussed later in this chapter.

Then there is the location of the auction house. Is it easy to get to? If the picture does not sell, will it be inconvenient to go and pick it up?

Another aspect to consider is the likelihood that your picture will get damaged whilst at the auctioneer's premises. There are auction houses where one can almost guarantee that the frame or the picture itself will suffer. One has only to observe how pictures are moved, stacked and handled during the sale in some auction houses, to realize that the likelihood of damage is quite considerable. What is less in doubt is that the picture will be lost, but it does happen. Clearly, at the top of the range of auction houses, the treatment meted out is generally careful and considerate.

Finally, user-friendliness, can also be an influence. There is still a strong macho image prevailing in some locations – more at the lower end and where the trade prevails, where the private punter can be made to feel very much the outsider. Other houses provide a certain amount of comfort – chairs, a buffet, easy payment facilities and staff whose opinions and advice one can solicit.

Reserves and Estimates

Recently, a colleague took an oil painting round the main London houses and received estimates of £2,000 to £3,000; £800; and £100–£150. The reason for the great differences was due to variations in opinion as to whether the painting was by the artist whose signature was on the painting or not. On another occasion, a sculpture was rated at £2,000 to £3,000 at one house because the artist's popularity had recently waned dramatically, and £20,000 to £25,000 at another, because they thought it had not.

This is a basic problem. For a range of painters whose work frequently appears at auctions, there is less difficulty in establishing a likely selling price range. Beyond this, you are dependent on the expertise of whoever you consult at the auctioneers. In London auction houses, there is generally a melee of people surging around the counter behind which are assistants who call up the appropriate expert, who either appears in due course or to whom the picture is taken. The decision is generally taken quickly unless the picture is of obvious interest and high value, when it will be proposed that it is retained for a more expert opinion. Experience indicates especially in London, that a lack of expertise, or alternatively, willingness to do a little research, sometimes prevails, and one has to be alert to this, for a good painting may be substantially undervalued. Evidence that this is so is the fairly frequent occurrence of opportunities to buy undervalued pictures at auction.

At the end of the day, all other things being equal, one probably leaves the picture with whichever auctioneer is most enthusiastic, seems to know what he or she is talking about and is willing to agree a reasonably high but realistic reserve.

Auctioneer's Discretion

Generally, reserves are agreed when the picture is entered for the sale on the 'Instructions-to-sell' form. Auctioneers reserve the right to decline an entry which in their opinion is subject to an excessive reserve. If you do not agree a reserve and insist on a higher one than the auctioneer is prepared to agree to, and the picture subsequently does not sell, you may find that the consequences are very onerous.

Frequently, the seller gives the auctioneer 10 per cent discretion. Some auctioneers reserve the right to sell below this 10 per cent discretion level, but, if they do so, some agree that the seller is entitled to the 10 per cent discretion price level.

So you have to decide whether to give the auctioneer discretion or not. This means that if you have agreed a reserve of, say, £500, the auctioneer can sell if the bidding only reaches £450. If the percentage is not clearly specified then you are giving the auctioneer greater latitude to accept a lower bid than £450. This may be interpreted as a little under £450. The way bidding goes, this may well be £420. You have to decide whether you are keen to sell. For example, you may have paid only £200 for the picture, so that £420 would not be too bad. However, you have to pay commission, insurance and possibly also for an illustration, not to mention the VAT on all of these charges, so that you may only finish up with about £320 – still quite a nice profit. But if you had originally paid £300, the initially attractive £500 reserve does not look so good if the auctioneer has unspecified discretion. In this situation one might argue against any discretion at all. Alternatively, with some auction houses, you can say how much you want in your hand after all charges have been paid, e.g. in this example, 'I want £400 after all charges.' Take note that many auctioneers specify in their conditions that all goods are put up for sale without reserve unless written instructions as to reserves are submitted before the sale.

The relationship between reserves and estimates has already been discussed in the previous section. The bottom estimate is often the reserve or the reserve less 10 per cent. The auctioneer will often argue for a low reserve, not just to make his job easier but also to attract several buyers who sense a bargain. If he is successful in so doing, the several buyers may push the price up to well beyond the upper estimate.

If you are too ambitious with your reserve you may find that your lot was bought in just below the reserve you agreed. If the trade knows that a picture hasn't sold, they also know that if it re-appears again, the reserve will be considerably lower. Second time round you are likely to get a good deal less than if you had had a more modest reserve, first time round. Much depends on whether you don't care whether you sell or not – or whether you want to get rid of the picture and transform it into cash.

Sales Commission

Sales commissions vary substantially. The range is from about 7½ per cent to 15 per cent. Some auction houses charge less for lots selling over a particular figure. For example, one auction house charges 10 per cent for lots selling over £500 and 15 per cent for lots selling under £500. Another charges 12½ per cent for lots selling over £500 and 15 per cent for lots selling under £500. Some make a minimum charge which can vary from £5 to £45. Some have no minimum charge. Some also make a handling charge – for example, £2 per lot. One auction house, which charges 12½ per cent, includes insurance and illustration charges.

However, commission rates are often negotiable. For example, it may be agreed that the rate will be 10 per cent even if the hammer price does not reach £1,000. There is frequently a lower rate for 'the trade' or for any vendor who consigns large volumes of goods to the auction house. Outside of the major London houses, it is often possible to negotiate lower rates, such as 7½ per cent.

Insurance Charges

Generally, unless the auctioneer is instructed otherwise, all goods held on the auctioneer's premises and in his custody will be held insured, for which the usual charge is 1 per cent of the gross amount realized but some auction houses charge 1½ per cent. It may be that the vendor's own insurance provides cover whilst his pictures are with an auctioneer, when it may be worth while instructing the auctioneer in writing that insurance is not required. However, most household contents insurance policies specifically exclude 'furniture store, sale room or exhibition'.

It should be noted that the insurance covers for theft but often with the proviso 'following forcible entry' and fire and water damage but not for accidental breakage or damage. Auctioneers generally refuse to accept responsibility for accidental damage unless it can be shown to be directly caused by the negligence of their employees. It is worth finding out just what you are paying for.

Buying-in Charges

If you are the seller, you are informed of any lots that have not sold. You then have to decide whether to remove the pictures from the sale room or to have them put up again at the next auction. Meanwhile you may have to pay a commission on the unsold items. What you may have to pay will depend on whether you have agreed a reserve with the auctioneer. If you have, the buying-in costs should be modest.

But if you have insisted on a higher reserve than the auctioneer thinks appropriate, you could be liable, for example, for half of the rate of commission calculated on the bought-in price. Many auction houses charge 5 per cent to 7½ per cent of the final bid. Come what may, there will also be insurance and illustration costs.

It is important to negotiate what you will pay, if anything, for bought-in items where there is an agreed reserve. (It is clear that a non-agreed reserve is not a good idea.) It is possible, in some circumstances and some auction rooms, to get agreement that no charge will be levied for unsold items but it has to be done before the sale. Outside of London, the charge for bought-in items is often a fixed sum such as £2–£3.

There is generally a short time limit within which the unsold items must be removed. In practice, there is usually some leeway but in London, if you delay, you can find that your pictures have been spirited away to some warehouse. Outside of London, there is generally more tolerance as to time limits, but often the small print is quite menacing if you fail to take action to deal with your unsold lots. For example, some houses say that unless the unsold lots are collected or instructions are given to reoffer them, they can be reoffered without reserve and all costs and charges will be deducted from the price obtained. In this situation you may well find that you owe the auctioneer money. One house gives you seven days to make up your mind as to what you want to do with the unsold items. If you do not comply, the lots will cease to be insured and they can be sold without reserve and charges will again be levied.

If the items are to be put up again at the next auction, you will probably incur further commission charges. If you live outside of London and put pictures into London salerooms, it is tempting, if they don't sell, to have them put up again. However, this may mean that you have to pay a further commission. It is possible, if this procedure goes unchecked, that you will finish up in debt to the auctioneers rather than getting something for your pictures. Often, but not always, when a picture reappears at the same auction, or even at another one frequented by the same buyers, it is harder to get such a good price second or third time round.

Sometimes, if the reserve is not reached, the auctioneer will say, 'See me afterwards'. Even if he doesn't, buyers will do so, to see if they can negotiate somewhere below the reserve. Remember, almost everything is negotiable, and when it is not withdraw from the fray if you are unhappy with what is unnegotiable.

Again, it is important to read and understand the small print and, if necessary, negotiate changes in your favour, confirmed in writing.

Catalogue Illustrations

Whilst many auctioneers' conditions say that the seller gives them full and absolute right to photograph and illustrate any lot placed with them for sale, in practice this is normally a matter for negotiation. The argument is usually that an illustration will enhance the price by drawing more bidders. This may or may not be so. On balance, you have to depend on the integrity of the advice given to you. The argument swings very much in favour, if agreeing to an illustration means that the auctioneer will also illustrate your lot in the advertisements he places for the auction sale in the press. The cost can vary from £25 to £90 for a black-and-white reproduction and £50 to £200 or more for a coloured illustration – plus, of course, VAT.

You should attempt to negotiate that you will only pay for the illustration if the sale is successful. If you cannot succeed in doing this, you may decide that the illustration charge means that the chances of selling at a profit are meagre and decline to illustrate. At the top end of the market, every picture is illustrated, so that refusal would give a very negative message to buyers. However, in the general run of sales about one picture out of every three are illustrated at the top end, about one in ten in the middle range and none at all at the lower end. An illustration does suggest to the buyer that the item is above the general run of the mill. The copyright of the illustration remains with the auction house.

Value Added Tax (VAT)

VAT is chargeable on the sales commission, insurance charges, buying-in charges, illustration costs and most other expenses. If you are selling a picture which is an asset of your business, you must disclose to the auctioneer whether you are registered for VAT and, if you are, the registered number of your business and whether you operate what is called 'the special scheme' or 'the margin scheme'. The margin scheme works on the principle that you pay VAT on the profit of selling and buying.

If you operate the margin scheme, then the way it works when buying and selling at auction is as follows. When you buy at auction, you pay the hammer price, the buyer's commission and the VAT on the buyer's commission. This is the cost of the purchase. You do not claim this VAT back. When you sell at auction, you receive the hammer price less the sale's commission, insurance and any other costs and less the VAT levied on these sales expenses. This is the income from the sale. You do not claim this VAT back.

You pay VAT on the difference between the income from the sale less the cost of the purchase. If you buy and/or sell other than at auction, you still pay VAT on the difference between the purchase cost and the sales income. You can, of course, reclaim the VAT you pay on restoration or framing costs. If you are not registered for VAT, none of this need concern you.

Tricks of the Trade

It is useful to be aware of the possible shenanigans that can occur at an auction sale, some of which have already been described in chapter 7. Most auctioneers have considerable integrity, and the success of their business depends on this being evident. However, not every buyer or seller is so motivated.

From the seller's point of view, any type of collaboration between buyers to avoid competition amongst them is disadvantageous. The form this might take has already been described in chapter 7. There is not much the seller can do about it, other than avoid auction houses where such collaboration seems to be rife.

Some sellers bid up their own pictures. This is only permissible on any lot, provided that the seller has not agreed to there being a reserve on the lot. If this is so, the seller runs the risk of having the picture knocked down to him and being saddled with paying both the sales commission and the buyer's premium. However, if there is a reserve, the procedure is illegal because otherwise the seller could bid and stop short of the reserve and thus encourage the bidding on his or her picture, without incurring the risk of buying it. It is possible for the seller to get someone else to bid, stopping short of the reserve, having been told what it is. This is clearly an action not to be advised because the intention is illegal. When you are buying at auction, it is as well to be aware that this may be going on, particularly if a 'ring' is operating.

Collecting the Unsold

Once again, it is worth emphasizing that the longer a picture remains with an auction house, the more likely it is to get damaged. This, coupled with the threat and possible reality of storage charges, makes it advisable to collect the unsold as soon after the sale as possible. You should make sure that it will be convenient for you to do this as part of your consideration when you choose the auction house to sell your picture.

Generally, you have to pay any costs incurred before you can collect the picture. These may include selling commission, insurance costs, illustration costs, buying-in charges; and VAT on all these and any other charges. The accounts department of the auction house may be inclined to charge everything even though you understood, for example, that you would not have to pay a buying-in charge. It is essential to agree all charges in advance of the sale; and often some of them are negotiable. Ideally, you should confirm the agreed basis of charges in writing, so that you are in a position to challenge the bill when it is presented to you for payment. If you have not done so, you may find yourself out of pocket.

Storage Charges

The rules governing storage charges vary from one auction house to another. Some auction houses are very tolerant and allow you to leave the pictures until the next auction sale. Others want you to remove them, but make no storage charges. Others cart your pictures off to a warehouse, charging perhaps £2 for the transport and £1.25 per day for storage.

A complication is that the storage charges are not always levied, even though the fine print says they will be. Again, the best thing to do is to discover what is custom and practice and also the location of the store, which may be somewhere quite different from where the auction house is located so that getting there may add even further expense to collection.

Summary

Someone who is just beginning to buy and sell pictures can often feel reassured that, even if he does buy badly, he can always get rid of his mistakes at auction. However, this is not always so. Really bad mistakes don't sell at all. Even if you can get the purchase hammer price at the sale auction, you may lose upwards of 30 per cent.

This also demonstrates that if you intend to make a living by buying at one auction and selling at another, you have to have a rough and ready rule to buy at least one third below your conservative estimate of the hammer price you think it will achieve when you sell. When you put all your other costs, such as travelling and interest charges, into the equation, you see that you must be looking to double the price when you sell. The mathematics of all this are given in Appendix 4 where formulas are given to enable you to calculate the selling price you need to achieve under a variety of conditions.

Otherwise, realize that the seller, as well as the buyer, has to be aware of reserves, costs and all the fine print, and the extent to which this is negotiable. Selling is the testing time and the profits and losses in your stock book will tell you whether you are making progress towards being a profitable dealer.

9 Choosing the Auction House and the Importance of Timing

Auction Houses

The UK, particularly England, is well provided with auction houses. There is a wide spectrum from the prestigious London houses to the village halls that hold once-in-a-while auctions.

In London, the four main houses – in alphabetical order – are Bonhams, Christie's, Phillips and Sotheby's. Christie's and Sotheby's vie with each other for being the front runner in the UK, and at both a multi-million price for a single picture is not unusual. These Central London houses, however, frequently have sales where prices extend from a few hundred pounds upwards to five figures.

However, each of these houses has a slightly down-market, but nevertheless prestigious, off-shoot, where the range of prices is more modest, although they do overlap at the top end, those prices being obtained at the main houses. Bonhams have such rooms at Lot's Road, Christie's at South Kensington, Phillips at Bayswater and Sotheby's at Billingshurst, West Sussex. South Kensington and Billingshurst tend to have works of higher prices and quality than do Lot's Road and Bayswater.

There are many other auction houses in London which

have more in common with those elsewhere in the UK. Bonhams and Phillips have a number of rooms around the country. Christie's hold auctions in Glasgow, Phillips in Edinburgh, both of which tend to be quite up-market.

Auction houses outside of London vary in prestige and the quality of pictures sold. Some are full of trade pictures – those that runners have been unable to place or have bought cheaply, some that galleries have had too long and some from galleries that have closed down. Several of the houses outside London have occasional prestigious sales interspersed with more run-of-the-mill ones. Others sell pictures along with furniture, jewellery, silver, etc.

The *Antiques Trade Gazette* provides each week, lists of auction sales for each day of the week for several weeks ahead. From this you can pick the local ones, arrange to attend and see what you think of them both for buying and selling.

Buying – Which Auction House?

If you are a collector and are seeking pictures by two or three artists, it is sensible to go to the locality where they painted and where there is a ready market for the paintings. However, although you may quickly find what you want, the prices will tend to be higher than if you search around in an area of the country where they are not well known. Some paintings will clearly sell better in London – for example, paintings by foreign artists or of foreign countries such as Italy, the Arab countries or Australia or of ethnic subjects.

Some auctioneers are very knowledgeable and scrupulous about authenticity. This is reassuring to the buyer but it means that the likelihood of finding something that has escaped the auctioneer's eye is fairly remote but by no means impossible. 'Sleepers' or 'snips' are more likely to be found in the less rigorous auction rooms in some of which the auctioneer might regard himself as limited to being an agent with no responsibility as to authenticity. Here, you are on your own and 'let the buyer beware' must certainly be in your mind.

If you go round the rooms, you may gain the impression that the prices in some rooms are higher than in others. Dealers will tell you, 'That is a good place to sell but not to buy.' However, so many factors affect what happens in a particular room on a given day that such broadly based advice is probably misleading. If you want to buy at bargain prices, there is really no alternative but to get into your mind what is cheap and what is expensive, having regard to all the factors covered in the previous chapters, and to go to a number of sales until what you want and the price you want to pay coincide.

Established auction houses are straight, honest and well conducted. Go off the beaten track and you may find practices that are not entirely commendable. Most auctioneers want to be well regarded by their clientele and therefore do their best to be fair and honest. However, it is not unreasonable to expect them to do all they can legitimately to get the best price.

There are many country sales where a wide variety of merchandise is sold, including pictures. It is natural, but often naive, to think that these should be good places to pick up a bargain. No doubt bargains are picked up at such sales from time to time, but those running them are often knowledgeable, and if they have anything of value, they telephone likely dealers and bidders. So it is often surprising, having found something interesting but perhaps a little damaged, and having discovered in the price books that the artist commands four figures at times, that far from getting it for a hundred or two, one never enters the bidding because the price goes beyond what you would expect in the more traditional sale room.

Some sale rooms 'push' a particular artist. I attended such

a sale room and identified an artist from a part of the UK which pays well for those from its native heath. There were several pictures in the sale and I expected them to sell for perhaps a hundred pounds or so. In fact, they fetched two or three thousand. The next day there was another sale not far away, where a picture by this artist was in the catalogue and there was no estimate against it, indicating that it was not expected to fetch more than £100. I thought I was on to something, but the trade had also been to the first sale and as the bidding, to the astonishment of everyone else in the room, approached four figures, I retired from the fray.

Over the next year or two, pictures by this artist fetched progressively higher prices in the sale room I had first attended. Then this sale room had a sale devoted almost entirely to the works of this artist. Needless to say, they didn't achieve exceptional prices, but they didn't do at all badly.

Selling – Which Auction House?

Choosing an auction house at which to sell is a bit like choosing an estate agent. Go to several and you will be quoted different prices. Do you go to the agent who is prepared to put your property on the market for a higher price than anyone else, or do you judge him irresponsible and choose someone whose estimated selling price seems more realizable? Other factors enter into it – the quality of the sales literature, the user-friendliness of the agent and the rate of commission. Compared with choosing the right place to sell a picture, selling a house is relatively easy.

The trouble starts as soon as you try to establish the selling price, and continues through the jungle of reserves, estimates, insurance, illustrations and which sale. These and other considerations have already been discussed in chapter 8. They are clearly all relevant to making the decision where to sell.

Then there is the practical problem of getting the pictures to the auction and picking them up again if they do not sell. Unless you live in central London, it is a nightmare getting close enough to the auction rooms without fear of being clamped or having one's car bodily removed. There are parking meters, but they are very expensive. If the pictures do not sell and you cannot get to the rooms for a few days, when you eventually do so, you may find they have been whisked off to some obscure-to-you part of the metropolis. All this argues in favour of local rooms if you are outside central London.

However, there are often good reasons for wishing to sell in London – for example, you may have foreign or ethnic pictures to sell or very valuable ones, when convenience, parking, etc., merit less consideration. Also, some of the London houses run specialist sales – for example pictures of dogs before the dog show, of marinescapes before the boat show and of flowers before the Chelsea Flower Show.

The Importance of Timing

The auction trade depends to a considerable extent on the retail trade, which experiences a succession of periods of good trade and of slackness. The pre-Christmas period is probably the most buoyant for most galleries, and the period immediately afterwards can also be good, as people spend gifts of money they have received. Business is then fairly quiet until the Easter holidays and springtime, when hope and optimism combine with redecorating and refurbishment to encourage purchases of pictures. The summer can be a good time for galleries in holiday resorts but otherwise, in the cities, it can be very quiet. Come the autumn, things begin to quicken once again.

Superimposed on this pattern is the economic cycle. Booms, which are followed by high interest rates, presage a period of depression but also of opportunity, as those with too many pictures bought at high prices on borrowed money are forced to sell. Periods of low interest rates and of recovery and boom lead to rising prices. Often the events that cause or foretell a change in the economy occur suddenly and can affect the art market.

Then there are the trends of fashion or of purchasers' preference. A particular artist will suddenly find favour and prices may move up sharply. This movement may be engineered by large galleries or a group of individuals or may be a natural phenomenon. An example was the boom in Swedish pictures that took place a few years ago, when the index rose from a few hundred to over twenty thousand and subsequently back to below five thousand.

Apart from the special events and factors mentioned above, the autumn is often a good time to sell as dealers stock up for the pre-Christmas period. Bad times for selling are good times for buying. Not infrequently, several sales occur on the same day in a particular locality or there is a big sale in London which attracts most of the dealers away from the country sale you are interested in. This can provide a good opportunity.

Summary

Choosing the auction house at which to buy is largely determined by what you want to buy, whether you are a collector or a dealer, and where you live. If you subscribe to *Thesaurus*, you will be able to find out where pictures you might be interested in are to be sold. Where to sell is often more problematical. Again, geography plays an important part and experience also helps as you discover what sells in particular locations. As to timing, avoid buying at the top and selling at the bottom of the market cycle. Unfortunately, this is what a great many people do not do, as a result of excess optimism followed later on by excess pessimism and an unhelpful bank manager.

10 Buying from and Selling to the Trade

Galleries

Galleries selling pictures range from the large prestigious ones in London and other art centres to the modest shop in a country village. They tend to group, in London, in a number of areas, perhaps the best known being New Bond Street/Bruton Street, Old Bond Street, Cork Street and St James's. Outside of London, there are concentrations of galleries in the Cotswolds, Bath, St Ives, Plymouth, Edinburgh and Glasgow. Many galleries specialize in particular artists – contemporary and the past.

A very good guide to the UK galleries is the magazine *Galleries*. This is a monthly and can often be picked up gratis from galleries, which subscribe to be included in the magazine.

The first section, 'New Shows Diary', lists in date order, exhibitions that are opening – by the name of the gallery and the artists being exhibited. The second section contains editorial – reviews and market analysis. The third section provides lists of galleries by geographical areas, which are numbered. For most locations, there is a street map so that it is simple to find a particular gallery. The name, address, telephone number and fax number of each gallery is given together with opening hours and details of current exhibitions. There is an index listing the specializations of various galleries, organized under a number of headings, such as 'aboriginal art', 'animals', 'Art Nouveau and Art Deco'. There is also an artist index, listing artists alphabetically and the galleries that exhibit their work. Finally, there is an alphabetical index of galleries cross-referenced to the geographical area number. Hence, for a particular gallery consult the gallery index, for a category of art turn to the specialization index, and to find work by a specific artist use the artist index.

Another useful guide is *The Corporate Art Buyer's Guide to Galleries*, which comes from the publishers of *Art Review*. This devotes a single page to each gallery, with an illustration, outline of the gallery's approach, list of artists exhibited, address, telephone and fax number, opening hours, price range, and the name of the gallery director.

Prices tend to be higher at the major London, Cotswold and Home Counties galleries, because of the high cost of rent, rates and staffing.

There are many minor galleries that sell modest prints or works by local artists. These are rarely places to buy anything other than decoration. But there will be exceptions and the occasional signed print or painting may, in years to come, turn out to have been a good buy.

Buying from a Gallery

It is essential for the collector or would-be dealer to visit as many galleries as possible. This provides the opportunity to see what is being sold as regards specialization, artist and price range and also to see good examples of the sort of pictures you may have decided to specialize in. The gallery owner or director will generally be happy to discuss pictures with you. Naturally he or she will hope that you will be in the market but knows that the ratio of sales to visits is quite small and will not be surprised if at the end of a discussion you find a gracious way to exit without any commitment.

In due course, one makes friends with a number of dealers and gallery owners. These people are putting considerable amounts of money at risk and are generally very skilled in many of the aspects covered in this book. They probably know more than the experts, and it is useful for you to find out their particular areas of specialization.

In the more up-market galleries, you will not always find the gallery owner or director readily accessible. Many have receptionists who may quote you prices but who cannot do much more than make general comments. Some flatter you by treating you as an experienced collector, others as if you had very little business being in the gallery. However, you can always ask for the director or someone near the top, and either they will come forth or one can find out how to make contact with them. If you are going to take the time of some of these more important people, some advance preparation may be advisable to ensure that you get the maximum benefit from the contact.

Many galleries in London and outside, will be prepared to act for you in a variety of ways. For example, you might ask them to look at something you have seen on view at an auction. They might already have seen it and in fact, be intending to buy it. Unless they have an immediate buyer for it, however, it is possible that they may be agreeable to buy it for you, and to arrange for its restoration and framing. On the other hand, they may warn you against it because of condition or doubts about authenticity and thus save you a good deal of money. There is always the risk that a dealer might put you off a purchase at auction for his own selfish reasons, but such dealers are generally soon found out and part of the skill you develop is to know whom you can trust.

All that has been said about buying at auction as regards quality, authenticity, framing, etc., also applies when buying from a gallery. It is only too easy, especially at private views when the wine flows, to disengage one's critical faculty. 'Buy what you like' is possibly a valid criterion provided that your judgement is unclouded and that you are not influenced by sales talk – 'She is charging £X for her paintings these days' or 'it is impossible to buy this artist any more' and so on. You can always go away and think about it. Most galleries will give you 'first refusal' while you do this.

Negotiation on price is often possible away from the more prestigious establishments. Generally, you will pay more to buy from a dealer – a lot more in the West End of London – than if you were to buy the same picture at auction. But, when comparing auction and dealer prices, it is important to be comparing like with like. Superb examples of anything, command very much higher prices than run-of-the-mill items, and, on the whole, dealers will be going for quality. Pictures will also be restored and framed, often expensively. It is not unreasonable to argue that a good dealer will buy well at auction and therefore his gallery price may not be much different from what you may have had to pay at auction if you lack his expertise. Also bear in mind that you will make mistakes at auction, the cost of which has to be added to the cost of your more successful purchases.

Some of the great collectors and collections have been built up by purchasing from knowledgeable dealers and galleries. One of the most famous of dealers, Ambroise Vollard provides a wonderful insight into the world of the gallery owner in his book *Recollections of a Picture Dealer* (*Souvenirs d'un marchand de tableaux*, translated from the French by Violet M. Macdonald). He dealt in the paintings of the Impressionists at the end of the nineteenth century. With hindsight one can understand but nevertheless be surprised, at the indecision of clients to pay anything more than a handful of francs for paintings that now command six or seven figures in dollars. He recollects how a customer turned down a Van Gogh painting in favour of the work of a painter who was popular at the time but has been little heard of since. Anyone taking his advice, even though they might have paid more than at auction, was bound to make a great deal of money over a lifetime. This reads across to today – the knowledgeable dealer can still put the collector into pictures which will appreciate in value.

Apart from getting advice as to what is the best picture to buy, you also get a 'guarantee' of authenticity. If a gallery is prepared to give such a guarantee, ask for it in writing. If the gallery is not prepared to do so, it throws doubt on the value of the 'guarantee' and on the expertise of the gallery. Also, have regard to the gallery's financial stability. Galleries disappear even in the best streets. Consumer protection legislation offers little protection if the gallery has gone into liquidation.

If you buy a picture which subsequently turns out to have been stolen, the picture will have to be returned to the legal owner. If you have bought from a reputable gallery, the money you paid for it will normally be refunded. However, you may have difficulty in getting your money back, if you have bought 'in the street' – for example, at a car boot sale. The law relating to stolen goods is complicated and the above is only intended to give the general drift. Legal advice should be sought in any particular case.

When you visit a gallery, be sure to leave a card or sign the visitors' book. This will ensure that you are informed about exhibitions, and you may get an invitation to a private view. Most galleries sell through exhibitions on their own premises, and, if you attend the private view early enough, you have the opportunity to take your pick of what is on offer.

Selling to a Gallery

Galleries sometimes buy from runners who themselves buy at auction. The runner has to pay the buyer's premium and VAT, has to pay for the use of his car at auction and to go to possibly several galleries to sell and has to make a profit. You would expect a runner to charge the gallery about 50 per cent above the auction price. Therefore you might think that you could do the same. However, the runner is probably more expert than you are at buying bargains. If they are buying from someone they do not know, it is my experience that most galleries expect to pay no more than the auction price and often rather less.

In fact, galleries and dealers are often looking to buy items for a fraction of the price for which they can sell them. They are not alone in this; after all, that is what most people are hoping to do, spurred on by such television programmes as the *Antiques Road Show*. This they most readily do when Joe Public is selling, be it a house clearance or boot sale or someone coming into the gallery to raise the wind. So the important thing when selling to a gallery is not to be confused with Joe Public. Rather one must be, or at least give the impression of being, trade.

It is no use thinking that the dealer will tell you how much what you are offering is worth. In other words, you cannot generally say, 'What will you give me for this?' unless you want to be taken for an inexperienced amateur. You have to have a clear idea as to what price you are going to ask and how far below this you are prepared to go.

After all, galleries only want to buy what they feel fairly certain they can sell. If what you have to offer does not come into this category, then they will generally advise you to go elsewhere.

If you buy at auction with the idea of selling to a gallery, the hammer price needs to be about half of what you reckon the gallery would expect it to be – so that you can sell round about the hammer price and make a profit. The gallery's expectation will come from seeing similar pictures selling at auction or from the price books.

Having bought at auction and wishing to sell at a profit, you will be weighing up what you might get at auction with the need to pay commission, insurance, etc.; the possibility of having to collect it, if it doesn't sell; and what a gallery will pay for it. It is important to make the correct choice of gallery, and this may emerge from the advice you might receive from a gallery that does not want your picture but might suggest other more suitable ones.

All that has been said about making friends and getting to know the owners or directors when buying from a gallery applies equally well when thinking about selling to them. Frequent visits will tell one what the gallery customers buy and hence what the gallery wants to buy.

Sale or Return Arrangements (SOR)

Many galleries operate a sale or return arrangement. You agree a price that you want in your hand and the gallery applies a margin to this to arrive at a selling price. Alternatively, the gallery may say '£X is the most I can get for this picture to move it quickly, and I don't want it otherwise. Our commission is Y per cent so you will get 100 per cent less Y per cent of £X if we sell it. Is that acceptable to you?' Once you have agreed to put the picture with a gallery there is generally a time limit, and when this is reached and the picture hasn't sold, you have to collect it. Galleries will often frame or arrange restoration as a preliminary or as part of an SOR deal.

Sometimes the SOR works and sometimes it doesn't. The gallery may forget to tell you that it has sold your picture and waits for you to call. Occasionally the gallery goes into receivership and it may be difficult to separate your picture from the receiver's stock. Anyway, the gallery is going to sell its own pictures before it pushes yours, unless you are paying a hefty commission. Commissions range from a modest 15 per cent to an immodest 50 per cent or more. All the time your picture is on SOR, you have capital tied up. If you are an active trader, you cannot afford too much SOR.

Buying at Fairs

There are many fairs where pictures are on sale, ranging from the most prestigious down to car boot sales. Many are antique fairs at which art dealers exhibit. They provide the opportunity to shop around. For many of the smaller dealers, fairs represent their shop windows. Details of the more important fairs are given in the *Antique Dealers' Gazette*. There are publications which list many of the smaller fairs, and the local press often gives information on car boot sales.

Many of the pictures on offer in the furniture and general bric-à-brac stalls of antique fairs are overpriced, inferior material aimed at the unwary general public, so many of which believe that the more you pay, the better is the product. How often you hear one of a couple say 'I don't care whether it is the right price or not – it is worth it to me and I want it.' – music to the dealer's ears! Nevertheless, it is on these stalls that the occasional find is made.

Reputable picture dealers have stands at antique fairs, and some of them work from their homes and do not have a gallery. Dealing with them is similar to dealing with a gallery. Putting on an exhibition at a fair is quite costly and bargains may be had at the end of the fair if the dealer has not sold very much.

Dealers and others often begin to arrive before the official opening time of the fair so as to be the first to spot bargains. To compete, you have to do the same. Some fairs also charge a higher entrance fee for the first hour or two. It has been said that queues form at some fairs as early as 4 a.m. and that buyers are being forced to arrive the night before and camp out in their cars to make sure they are first off the starting-line. Inevitably, dealing sometimes starts from one estate car to another before the fair opens. In indoor fairs, trading often takes place between exhibitors before the fair opens to the public. Where these practices are common, you are unlikely to find bargains because they will all have been snapped up before you arrive. Some fairs have banned inter-dealer trading and these are the ones that might merit your attention – but you will still need to arrive a little before the opening time.

The more prestigious fairs are aimed at an international market and are good places to see a large number of excellent pictures, but they are not necessarily the best places to buy.

Selling at Fairs

It is not encouraged to take pictures to a fair and blatently attempt to sell them to exhibitors. However, it is possible to put a few pictures in the boot of the car and to persuade one or two exhibitors to come into the car park to look at them. It is something one can sometimes arrange in advance and is useful if the fair is near you and the dealer you want to show your pictures to is from afar and is exhibiting at the fair.

You can, of course, take a stand and become an exhibitor. Many dealers work from home, have stands at local fairs and markets, and sometimes do very well. From modest beginnings, one can move up market. It has the advantage over selling at auction or to dealers, that you can charge a retail price. Presentation is important and pictures have to be clean and well framed. Exhibiting at fairs is also a way of getting known. You can hand out cards and encourage people to sign the visitors' book so that you can develop a mailing list.

Buying at Exhibitions

Probably the most famous exhibition in the UK is the Summer Exhibition held annually at the Royal Academy in Piccadilly, London. A wide variety of pictures are shown and are on sale at prices ranging from a few hundred pounds to ten thousand or more. You can be sure of being invited to the private view if you are a Friend of the Royal Academy, which you can become by taking out a subscription. The private view gives you the best opportunity to buy a picture by a contemporary artist, who may also be a Royal Academician. I am old enough to remember pictures I could have bought forty years ago from the RA for a few hundred pounds that are worth hundreds of thousands of pounds now. The opportunity is still there to buy works of exceptional quality from the Summer Exhibition.

Numerous exhibitions are held throughout the UK with a diversity of themes and with works of a single artist or of groups and pictures are on sale at many of them. Details appear in the arts pages of the Sunday broadsheets and in the art magazines.

Other Places to Buy and Sell Pictures

Many antique shops buy and sell pictures – some important in their own right, others as furnishings. There are also antique centres where a hundred or so dealers and units are congregated together, some of which are art dealers. You generally have less safeguard as regards authenticity when buying from these places compared with the long-established gallery. There is less expertise and such dealers often move from place to place, so if you do buy from them, it is as well to depend on your own judgement and knowledge. Most of these shops are selling to the non-expert public, and some of what is on sale is not always what it seems. This is particularly so with pictures. But it is wrong to generalize and, whilst advocating caution, you can generally pick out and make friends with dealers of integrity and knowledge.

Shops with bric-à-brac or even 'junk' may have something of interest. Some good finds have often been made at such places. The charity shops used also to be possible hunting-grounds for the bargain hunter, but these days they mostly have the help of the local dealers, and anything of any value goes elsewhere.

Car boot sales are the bottom end of the fair market. Pictures appear on the *Antiques Road Show* from time to time that have been bought for a few pounds at a car boot sale so that nowadays dealers and public rake through them. It is necessary to arrive before the sale opens if you want to find a bargain because you will not be alone. Again, it is a lottery but good fun, particularly if you believe events of low probability are likely to happen to you.

Pictures are also bought and sold through advertisements in home furnishing magazines, local papers and 'freebies' by private persons or dealers in disguise. Usually, much that is on offer is either overpriced or of little value. There is always the possibility of making a find, but there is the expense of time and money, so that it is a gamble. These outlets can be worth trying if you have pictures to sell that are known to be popular in a particular district. They need to be offered at well below the retail price.

Buying Direct from the Artist

Although the majority of artists sell through galleries or agents, some do sell from their own studios. Two such, Robert Lenkiewicz and Stuart Armfield, work in studios on the Barbican in Plymouth. Their work is also sold in galleries and appears sometimes at auction. The advantage of buying from the artist is that you can discuss with him or her the range of work and can gain an understanding of how the artist paints. It is always possible that you can buy more cheaply this way.

An alternative is to become an agent for a new and as yet undiscovered artist. This can be an interesting and exciting but possibly expensive and financially unrewarding venture into the unknown. The budding artist is generally impecunious so that you may have to carry the cost of framing, arranging exhibitions and even supplying materials. This can run into many thousands of pounds. However, if you have found a genius – a future David Hockney or Lucien Freud – you might eventually make a fortune, provided the artist repays you for putting him on the map, by staying with you. Even if he doesn't, you can have the satisfaction of having made a contribution to twentieth- or possibly twenty-first century art.

Summary

If you have plenty of money and wish to collect and keep your pictures for the long term, then buying from a reputable gallery is a good idea. The gallery directors should be able to put you into sound investments which are consistent with your taste and aesthetic judgment. Selling to a gallery is more for the runner or trader, but even if you are not one of these, it might often be a good alternative to selling at auction. Buying at fairs and exhibitions should be undertaken with the same caution as has been advocated when buying at auction.

11 Taking Care of Pictures

Housing

Pictures are usually stored in houses or galleries but from time to time spend some time in auction house stores and in various forms of transport. It is amazing how resilient they can be, often being abandoned in lofts or roof-spaces, only to be discovered a generation later, having appreciated substantially in the interim.

Works on paper are clearly more vulnerable than oils on canvas. Direct sunlight will fade many colours and will darken and weaken the cullulose fibre of the paper. If works on paper are not mounted, i.e. backed with a paper board, then every time they are handled there is a good chance that the paper will be creased or kinked. Unmounted water-colours, in thin plastic envelopes, are frequently to be seen at auction previews, guarded by an assistant. On requesting to see one of them, the assistant often grabs it with one hand between finger and thumb and passes it over, causing damage which is very difficult to repair. They are not always in plastic envelopes and it is not appreciated that fingers can be dirty, greasy or at best exude a certain amount of harmful acid. If an unmounted painting on paper is to be handled, two hands should be used in such a way the paper is never kinked or threatened with creasing and, ideally, gloves should be worn.

Water-colours and works on paper should have a backing mount board made of pure rag fibre, free of acid, to which the painting is attached by a small tab or hinge. A similar board, often called a 'mount', is cut to form a window and border to fit over the picture and the backing board. Boards from which mounts may be cut can be obtained in a variety of colours and are often embellished, for example, with wash lines. The term 'neutral or acid free', often used with reference to backing and mount boards, infers a neutral pH value of 7. However, to provide greater safety against discoloration, archival quality boards are being increasingly used which are alkaline with a pH value of not less than 8. The picture should then be framed, with a glass front and a firm backing. The glass of the frame should fit tightly so that dirt cannot get in and the backing should be sealed so that as far as possible the painting is in an airtight box. It is essential that the glass is held away from the surface of the painting by an adequately thick window mount.

Dampness is the cause of mould growth. Well-framed pictures in a centrally heated environment are not at risk but even they can deteriorate if put into a cold attic or roof space.

Oil paintings are more robust but are clearly better protected if adequately framed. Most are not covered with glass, but the glass does provide protection. However, if the painting is stored in a damp atmosphere the glass may encourage the growth of mould. Dirt or dust damages oil paintings and should be removed from time to time by dusting with a soft paintbrush.

Pictures do fall down due to inadequate fixings into the wall. It is convenient to knock a nail into plaster but the plaster can give way, the nail tilts and the picture crashes down. The wall should be plugged and a screw inserted to give a good fixing. Otherwise, the other main source of damage to the picture is the rusting of the brass wire for hanging (actually steel wire with a very thin covering of brass).

Handling

Pictures are fragile objects which can easily be damaged by any sharp objects such as a fingernail or coat-button. Works on paper are particularly vulnerable. Care should be taken when picking up framed paintings under glass. Pictures covered with glass can be quite heavy, and the frame may not be strong enough to allow you to pick up the picture by the fingers of one hand while holding the top rail of the frame. The same is true of framed oil paintings. Although it is more awkward, pictures should be held with both hands. Frames are frequently damaged by being knocked when carried through doorways or put into the boots of cars or kicked as they lie propped against a wall.

Packing pictures is a job requiring skill and thought. For transport in the car boot or estate car, it is best to wrap the pictures in such things as old blankets or counterpanes readily obtained from the local jumble sale. Plenty of packing should be used, and the pictures should be stacked in a way that prevents their movement. Hooks and eyes are a frequent cause of damage when pictures are stacked, and these should be removed. For transport by carrier or in a van, pictures should be wrapped in bubble wrap well secured with self-adhesive tape, with special precautions being taken with the corners. Usually they can be stored upright, which reduces the possibility of damage provided they are well-secured.

Security

Having acquired a number of pictures, it is necessary to consider security. Losses to your stock can occur at your own house or business premises or if you are or someone else is transporting pieces either with your own car or van or with a hired one. Losses can also occur at auction or if you have pictures on sale or return at another gallery.

The first and obvious, but often overlooked, tenet is to take care not to leave your pictures in an insecure environment. An auction sale is one such place, where after the sale you may sometimes see pictures propped against the outside of the owner's car whilst he is still inside the rooms. Next, one has to consider the security arrangements at the place where most of your pictures are kept. This may be your home, and if you have valuable pictures you may consider installing some form of intruder detection and alarm system or put bars on the ground-floor windows, or do both. The other form of protection is to take out insurance.

Insurance

Most households have contents insurance, and many policies cover relatively inexpensive items from theft, storm or flood, burst pipes and oil leaks. They generally do not cover damage by vermin, insects and mildew but often cover movement of the property by vehicle or by professional removal contractors. It is usual for the insurers to require you to disclose items exceeding £1,000 in value, and if you make a claim you will either have to produce the purchase document or a written valuation. It may be a good idea to get quotations from brokers who specialize in insuring pictures. For example, they can arrange for immediate coverage from the moment you purchase a new item.

You can get free verbal valuations by taking your pictures to a number of auction houses, and this may be a good preliminary to paying for written valuations. You may be surprised by the wide variations quoted, but remember that the auctioneer's free valuation is an estimate of what the picture will sell for at auction. If your insurance is 'new-for-old', then the valuation needs at least to reflect what would have to be paid to replace your pictures by buying from a gallery. It is usual to add a little extra to this figure as a factor of safety and to allow for inflation.

Consequently, the insurance value may be many times the auction price. A news item in the *Antiques Trade Gazette* (3 Feb 1996; no. 1223), illustrates this point. A Tiffany bracelet was valued at £8,000 for insurance purposes. The bracelet was subsequently stolen, and a replica from Tiffany's cost £38,345 to make. A case was brought against the valuers, and £26,149 was awarded by the courts to the owners of the bracelet. The judge upheld the owners' decision to order the replacement through Tiffany's rather than have a facsimile of similar standard made more cheaply elsewhere. You should consider how this applies to the valuation of your own pictures, and it is a cautionary message to you if you undertake professional valuation yourself.

Ewart Angus, in a letter to the *Antiques Trade Gazette*, has written: 'A valuation is subjective and highly discretionary. As such, it affords as little or as much comfort and authority as it bestows in the mind of the eventual seeker of its advices.' One can only hope that whatever valuations you may have paid for will give enough comfort to the insurance company for them to pay up if you have to claim.

Valuations for insurance are carried out by most auction houses and by many galleries. The costs vary, but 1–1½ per cent of the value of the pictures plus VAT is normal, with possibly a minimum fee charged. It is sensible to negotiate that only your valuable pictures will be valued.

Advertisements of pictures that have been stolen appear every week in the *Antiques Trade Gazette* and it would be wise to glance at these in case you see them come up at auction. New Scotland Yard has an Art and Antiques Squad (confidential telephone line 0171-230 4974). *Trace* magazine has a circulation of 20,000 in 170 countries and has built up a listing of over 40,000 stolen items. An electronic version has now been developed to enable up-to-the-minute searching.

Security Arrangements

The building within which pictures are housed should be physically secure. Many devices are available to thwart burglars, two out of three of whom gain access through a window. Window locks are therefore essential. Doors should be secured with a security deadlock, which can only be opened with a key. If very valuable pictures are hung in a room downstairs, windows should be barred. Secondary glazing can also provide some security.

Pictures can be secured to the wall by mirror plates but these can readily be removed using a screwdriver. There are security fixings which use special screws which are screwed into plugs in the wall, or directly into the wall, if it is of an appropriate material for this to be done. Metal housings are screwed to the back of the picture frame. The ends of the screws engage with the housings using a special key. The pictures cannot be removed from the wall without knowledge of how the fixings work and without the special key.

Electronic surveillance and protection is now generally recommended and used for the security of works of art. The basic components are movement detectors and door contacts. For the average household, infra-red movement detectors or PIRs are installed in the main rooms where valuable pictures are hung. It is also usual to fit door contacts on external doors. For particularly valuable pictures, individual microswitches and sensors can be fitted and the picture has to be secured to the wall.

These systems can either be hard-wired (i.e. the various components are joined by wires) or radio-linked (i.e. the components are linked by radio transmitters and receivers). The hard-wired systems are more expensive to install and also have unsightly wiring. There are quite cheap radio-linked systems which you can install, but they have a tendency to be set off by accident from radios of ambulances, police cars etc. The expensive high-class radio-linked systems are very good.

In a gallery situation with a line of pictures, an active infra-red beam can be installed in front of them. Four beams are usually installed, all of which have to be broken before the alarm goes off. This enables a certain amount of movement in front of the picture but the picture cannot be removed from the wall without all the beams being broken at the same time. There is also a device which is of assistance to protect galleries open to the public, if an alarm is triggered. This fills the room with a dense mist such that you cannot see your hand six inches away from your face. The intention is that the thief will not be able to escape with his loot. In due course the mist clears and no residue is left behind.

These electronic systems – hard-wired or radio-linked – can be connected to a control centre, so that if the premises are broken into when they are empty, the key holders are notified and so may be the police. For hard-wired systems, there are arrangements to alert the control centre if the telephone lines are cut. With radio-controlled systems, this is not a problem.

Some insurance companies give a discount if an electronic alarm system is installed. However, if you accept this discount, you will generally not be covered if the alarm system is not active.

Summary

Pictures have an amazing ability to survive, considering how delicate many of them are. There is really no excuse to treat them badly – they need tender loving care; and not only the pictures but the frames that protect them.

Every time pictures are moved there is a risk of damage. This is especially true if they fail to sell and journey through a succession of auction houses. If your pictures start off clean and newly framed, it is exasperating to find them acquiring scratches and defects, but it may not matter too much if they were in none too pristine condition at the outset and are aimed at the trade buyer.

The other hazard is theft. It is only too easy to think that it will never happen, but as it well might it is prudent to introduce burglar alarms and adequate insurance in your house, gallery or store.

12 Financial Considerations

The amount of capital you need to get into the business of buying and selling pictures depends on what you intend to achieve. If you are just going to take a very modest stance, wandering around the local shops and markets, hoping to pick up bargains, the costs can be minimal, but, unless you are very lucky, so will be the opportunities to make a profit.

If you have plenty of money and do not wish to get too involved in the technical and academic aspects of buying and collecting, you can choose one or two galleries and rely on them to sell you pictures that are right and that should at least keep their value. Inspection of the movement of the international art auction market (see fig. 1 above) shows accelerating appreciation from 1981/2 to 1989/90 followed by a dramatic fall and a slow recovery since 1991/2. As with most forms of investment, you can argue whether it is a good or bad form of investment depending on the years you choose to start and end the comparison. Historically, over a long period of time, investment in the art market has had the potential to be at least a good hedge against inflation. This will probably be so for the future provided you buy when the market is subdued and avoid buying near the top of a boom.

Trading

If you want to make money – and run the risk of losing it –

you will probably turn towards trading, by buying and selling in the short term.

The overheads (i.e. the 'fixed' money cost, independent of how much trading you do), include:

Some form of transport – a car, estate wagon or van. You may reasonably argue that you need a car anyway, so it is probably sensible to allocate some proportion of the capital cost and depreciation cost to trading.

Somewhere to store pictures safely. You may have a larger house than you need because you are trading in pictures and therefore should allocate some proportion of its value. If you have a shop or gallery that you own, this represents capital employed; alternatively, you may rent and pay rates. There is also insurance and the cost of security to be considered.

The amount of money you will have tied up on average for trading.

The cost of reference books, magazines and subscriptions.

The variable trading costs include:

The cost of transport (e.g. petrol, maintenance, packaging).

Administrative costs – computer, secretarial help, telephone, fax, post, photocopying, marketing literature and accounting.

The actual costs of buying and selling – premiums, insurance and VAT.

To illustrate the economics involved, an example might be:

Capital cost: £20,000, which at 10% costs £2,000.

Variable costs working from home, excluding buying and selling: for example, 45 auctions and 25 selling missions per year, the average cost of which is £50 for each of the 70 journeys, totalling £3,500.

Administrative costs: £1,500.

These costs add up to £7,000, or the average of £155.56 per auction visit. In other words, you have to make a profit, after tax, of £156 every time you buy at auction. If you want to gross £15,000 per year, for example, and you reckon to make 25% gross profit on buying and selling, then you have to deal in £28,000 of pictures to cover costs and a further £60,000 to make the gross profit – £88,000 in all, or about £2,000 per auction.

These calculations are not very refined, but they give some idea of what is involved in trading. They explain why dealers cannot live on sleepers alone but have to have volume. However, you and they might consider it more sensible to go to fewer sales and to buy fewer, but more expensive, pictures. Making £25 on a picture priced at £100 is very satisfying but is really not worth the trouble. You may use your own figures in the calculations above to see how you can best operate profitably.

Appendix 1

Useful Addresses

Art Magazines

Antiques Trade Gazette
17 Whitcomb Street, London WC2H 7PL
Tel. 0171-930 4957 Fax 0171-930 6391 E-mail metro-press-ltd@bbcnc.org.uk

Apollo (monthly)
29 Chesham Place, London SW1X 8HB
Tel. 0171-235 1998

Art Monthly (monthly)
Suite 17, 26 Charing Cross Road, London WC2H ODG
Tel. 0171-240 0389

Art Review (monthly)
Art Review Ltd, Hereford House, 23–24 Smithfield Street, London EC1A 9LB
Tel. 0171-236 4880 Fax 0171-236 4881
(informative and accessible insight into exhibitions throughout the UK)

Burlington Magazine (monthly)
Burlington Magazine Publications Ltd, 14–16 Dukes Road, London WC1H 9AD
Tel. 0171-388 1228

Contemporary Art (quarterly)
P.O. Box 406, Southampton S014 6ZB
Tel. 01703 672006
or
Freepost BS7966, Brooklands Mailing Services, Bristol BS2 9BR
(coverage of established artists and galleries and promotion of emerging talent)

The Fine Art File
Waterhouse & Dodd, 110 New Bond Street, London W1Y ORJ
Tel. 0171-491 9293 Fax 0171-491 9669

Irish Arts Review
22 Crofton Street, Dun Laoghaire, Co. Dublin, Ireland
Tel. 010 353 1 2808415 Fax 010 353 1 2808309

Modern Painters (quarterly)
Universal House, 251–255 Tottenham Court Road, London W1P 9AD
Tel. 0171-580 5618

RA Magazine (quarterly)
Friends of the Royal Academy of Arts, Piccadilly, London W1V ODS
Tel. 0171-439 7438 Fax 0171-287 9023

Addresses of Organizations Referred to in the Text

Chapter 1:

Art Price Index, Art Reference Books International of London, DMA Publicity House
9 Stanley Centre, Dept 11, Kelvin Way, Crawley, West Sussex RH10 2SE
Tel. 01293 541 511 Fax 01293 562 996

Art Sales Index, Art Quest & ASI Enquiry Service
Art Sales Index Ltd, 1 Thames Street, Weybridge, Surrey KT13 8JG
Tel. 01932 856426 Fax 01932 842482
E-mail: ASI@GLOBALNET.co.UK

Mayer's *International Auction Records* (see under Bénézit and Thieme–Becker below)

Thesaurus
Thesaurus Group Ltd, Mill Court, Furrlongs, Newport, Isle of Wight P030 2AA
Tel. 01983 826000 Fax 01983 826201

Chapter 2:

Antique Collectors' Club Ltd
5 Church Street, Woodbridge, Suffolk IP12 1DS
Tel. 01394 385501 Fax 01394 384434

Art Review
Hereford House, 23–24 Smithfield Street, London EC1A 9LB
Tel. 0171-236 4880 Fax 0171-236 4881

Ashmolean Museum
Beaumont Street, Oxford, Oxon OX1 2PH
Tel. 01865 278000/278010 01865 2781018

Banca dell'Arte
Unit 10, 535 Kings Road, London SW10 0SZ
Tel. 0171-349 8771 Fax 0171-349 8772
E-mail 100716.2213@compuserve.com

Bénézit and Thieme–Becker
Hilmarton Manor Press, Calne, Wiltshire SN11 8SB
Tel. 01249 760208 (or other major art booksellers)
(dictionaries of artists who have exhibited at various academies)

Dictionary of British Artists, Working 1900–1950
Eastbourne Fine Art, 9 Meads Street, Eastbourne, East Sussex, BN20 7QY
Tel. 01323 25634

Imperial War Museum
Lambeth Road, London SE1 6HZ
Tel. 0171-416 5000 Fax 0171-416 5374

National Army Museum
Royal Hospital Road, London SW3 4HT
Tel. 0171-730 0717 Fax 0171-823 6573

National Gallery
Trafalgar Square, London WC2N 5DN
Tel. 0171-839 3526

National Maritime Museum
Romney Road, Greenwich, London SE10 9NF
Tel. 0181-858 4422 Fax 0181-312 6632

National Portrait Gallery
St Martin's Place, London WC2H OHE
Tel. 0171-306 0055

Royal Academy of Arts
Burlington House, Piccadilly, London W1V 0DS
Tel. 0171-439 7438 Fax 0171-434 0837

Victoria and Albert Museum
Cromwell Road, London SW7 2RL
Tel. 0171-589 6371

Westminster Reference Library
St Martin's Street, London WC2H 7HP
Tel. 0171-798 2038 Fax 0171-798 2040

Who's Who in Art
The Art Trade Press Ltd, 9 Brockhampton Road, Havant, Hants

Witt Library of the Courtauld Institute of Art (University of London)
Somerset House, The Strand, London WC2R 0RN
Tel. 0171-873 2526

Chapter 5:

The Bonhams Directory
Kyle Cathie Ltd, 3 Vincent Square, London SW1P 2LX

Chapter 9:

Bonhams
Montpelier Street, London SW7 1HH
Tel. 0171-393 3900 Fax 0171-393 3905

Bonhams Chelsea
65-69 Lots Road, London SW10 ORN
Tel. 0171-393 3900 Fax 0171-393 3906

Christie's
8 King Street, St James's, London SW1Y 6QT
Tel. 0171-839 9060 Fax 0171 839 1611

Christie's South Kensington
85 Old Brompton Road, London SW7 3LD
Tel. 0171-581 7611 Fax 0171-321 3321

Christie's Scotland
164–166 Bath Street, Glasgow G2 4TG
Tel. 0141-332 8134 Fax 0141-332 5759

Phillips
101 New Bond Street, London W1Y OAS
Tel. 0171-629 6602 Fax 0171-491 1609

Phillips West Two
10 Salem Road, Bayswater, London W2 4DL
Tel. 0171-229 9090 Fax 0171-792 9201

Sotheby's
34–35 New Bond Street, London W1A 2AA
Tel. 0171-408 5129, 5130 or 5458 Fax 0171-491 2631

Sotheby's
Summers Place, Billingshurst, West Sussex RH14 9AD
Tel. 01403 783933 Fax 01403 785153

Chapter 10:

The Corporate Art Buyer's Guide to Galleries
Art Review, 20 Prescott Place, London SW4 6BT
Tel. 0171-978 1000   Fax 0171-978 1102

Galleries
Barrington Publications, 54 Uxbridge Road, London W12 8LP
Tel./Fax 0181-740 7020

Chapter 11:

Trace
Trace Publications Ltd, 38 New Street, Barbican, Plymouth PL1 2NA
Tel. 01983 826000   Fax 01983 826201

Appendix 2

Some Aids to Dating a Picture

If a picture is in original condition and in the original frame, this is a great help in estimating its age. Brown-paper backings of works on paper can be made to look as if the picture has never been removed from its frame, when, in fact, it has been. Old paper and nails can be used to make a modern painting look old. However, if it is claimed that the painting is old, the first question to ask yourself is whether it looks its proper age or looks as if it were painted yesterday. Unfortunately, because so much cleaning and restoration – which includes overpainting – occurs, old paintings can now look quite new. All this adds up to the fact that this is not an exact science and that you have to aim to get it right many more times than you get it wrong.

However, the following are further tips to dating, in addition to the ones concerning galleries and exhibition labels already mentioned in the text.

Works on Paper

Any sheet of paper which measures more than 135 cm by 79 cm cannot have been produced before 1772.

Mill numbers appear on paper only from the early

nineteenth century to 1851. Dates were necessary for tax purposes only from 1794 to 1811. A paper that has the mark 'J. Whatman Turkey Mill' is post-1794.

By 1840 the following drawing papers were available:

Demy	20″	by	15¼″
Medium	22¾″	by	17½″
Royal	24″	by	19″
Super-royal	27¼″	by	19½″
Imperial	30″	by	22″
Elephant	28″	by	21″
Columbia	35″	by	23½″
Atlas	34″	by	26″
Double Elephant	40″	by	27″
Grand Emperor	65″	by	47″
Antiquarian	53″	by	31″
Antiquarian (extra large)	56″	by	38″

Bristol Drawing paper and Card Boards
Vellum
More Cartridge for Landscape
Rough-grained Cartridge
Tinted Drawing Papers for Crayons

(The above information is taken from *The Artist's Craft: A History of Tools, Techniques and Materials* (1985) by James Ayres, originally published in *The Art of Painting Portraits, Landscapes, Animals, Draperies, Satin, &c., in Oil Colours* (1840) by John Cawse.)

Oil Paintings

The lines of weft and weave in canvases of the eighteenth century or earlier do not run in straight lines but tend towards the edges to go in fairly even waves that have their crests in line with the nails at the edge. Stout twill canvas was used by English portrait painters in the late eighteenth century. The grain often runs diagonally. Hand-made nails indicate a work of the eighteenth or early nineteenth century.

Seventeenth-century craquelure tends to be fine and is evenly distributed over the surface of a picture. Eighteenth-century craquelure tends to be more irregular, widely spaced and larger.

Trade marks on the back of canvases can help to date a picture. In his book, James Ayres gives the following example from the firm of Winsor & Newton:

1832	Winsor & Newton established at 38 Rathbone Place, London
1841–57	Appointment to Queen Victoria and Prince Albert
1857–61	Appointment to Queen Victoria and Prince Consort
1861–63	Appointment to Queen Victoria
1863–1901	Appointment to Queen Victoria and Prince and Princess of Wales
1878	Address changed from Rathbone Place, London, to Rathbone Place, London, W.
1882	Incorporated as Winsor and Newton Ltd
1901–10	Appointment to King Edward VII
1901–1925	Appointment to Queen Alexandra
1919–1935	Appointment to King George V
1911–1953	Appointment to Queen Mary
1917	Address changed to Rathbone Place, W.1
1939	Address changed to London, England
1951	Commencement of coding:

First letter = month (A–L)
Second letter = year (A = 1952, B = 1953, etc.)
Third letter = internal identification

Appendix 3

Check-list for Viewing a Picture

SALE...DATE..................

LOT NO. ....DESCRIPTION...

....

ARTIST...............................PERIOD.............................

ESTIMATE..............RESERVE...................INTEREST...................

WATER-COLOUR/PRINT

	NONE	A LITTLE	QUITE A LOT	A LOT
CONDITION - FOXING				
BURN MARKS				
SCUFFING				
DAMAGE/TEARS				
FADING				
WORM HOLES				

ESTIMATED COST OF REPAIR/RESTORATION ....

OIL

	NONE	A LITTLE	QUITE A LOT	A LOT
CONDITION - CRACKS				
DAMAGE/TEARS				
BLOOM				

CANVAS..................PANEL..................BOARD.......................
AGE/MAKER'S MARK RE ABOVE..
LINED - COMPO..............WAX..................STRIP......................

ESTIMATED COST OF REPAIR/RESTORATION ....

SIGNATURE - YES/NO....IF YES, AUTHENTIC - YES/NO....FROM EXPERIENCE.........
FROM SIGNATURE BOOK.....AUCTION HOUSE OPINION.....PROVENANCE...............

FRAME - DESCRIPTION..

DAMAGE...

VERSO - LABELS AND INSCRIPTIONS..

BIOGRAPHICAL ARTISTS' NOTES..

PRICE BOOK INFORMATION...

GALLERY/DEALER PRICE...

POTENTIAL BUYERS...

DECISION...

Appendix 4

Calculations for Buying and Selling at Auction

Having bought a picture at auction, it is useful to be able to calculate what the selling price should be to break even or to make a given percentage of profit. Equally, if you have a buyer who is prepared to pay an agreed amount, you need to be able to calculate what the hammer price at auction needs to be to show you a given margin.

For example, the hammer price of a picture you have bought at auction is £500. You think you can sell it at a profit at another auction house. What does the hammer price need to be to give you a gross profit of 25 per cent (before VAT or tax)? Or you have a purchaser for a picture who is willing to pay £600 for it. What does the hammer price need to be at auction to show you a gross profit of 20 per cent?

In all the calculations below relating to the hammer price, it is necessary to round the price up or down to the next practical bid interval price. For example bidding may go in the sequence: £500; £520; £550; £580; £600. If you calculate a hammer price of, say, £564, you have to round this up to the next interval, i.e. £580 or down to the previous interval, i.e. £550.

Buying at auction

If the hammer price is £500, the buyer's premium 15 per cent and VAT 17½ per cent, then the buying cost is £588.

If the buyer's premium is 10 per cent, the buying cost is £559.

If you have a client with whom you can agree a firm selling price for a picture which you are going to buy at auction, you need to work out the buying hammer price. Say the client is willing to pay £500 and you want 20 per cent gross profit and you are going to an auction house where the buyer's premium is 15 per cent, then you have to limit your bidding to £354 – in practical terms, £350.

Selling at auction

If the hammer price was £500, the commission rate 10 per cent and the insurance 1 per cent, then the sales income is £435.50.

If the commission rate is 15 per cent and insurance 1½ per cent, the sales income is £403.

Breaking even: What should the selling hammer price be to break even? Then the buying cost equals the sales income. If the buying hammer price is £500, the buyer's premium is 15 per cent, the sales commission and insurance is 11 per cent, then the selling hammer price to break even is £675. If there is an illustration charge of say £40, which becomes £47 with VAT, the selling hammer price for break even becomes £729.

Making a profit: In the example immediately above, if you want to make a gross profit of 20 per cent, the selling hammer price needs to be £810. Or with a £40 illustration cost, the selling hammer price needs to be £875.

If you have bought privately or from a gallery etc. you may

need to know the hammer price you need to make a profit, if you are going to sell at auction. If you have bought at £500, with a sales commission and insurance charge of 11 per cent and a gross profit of 20 per cent, the sales hammer price needs to be £689, i.e. probably £700 as this will be the next bid interval hammer price; or the lower bid interval price of £680, if you are prepared to get a little less than 20 per cent. With an illustration cost of £40, the sales hammer price needs to be £743, say £750.

When you estimate the selling hammer price, watch out for the auctioneer's 10 per cent discretion. In other words, selling hammer prices need to be increased by 11 per cent (or more accurately, divided by 0.9). So the break even reserve above without the illustration charge becomes £750 and with the illustration charge, £810 (£820 hammer price). The 20 per cent gross profit sales hammer reserve becomes £765 – say £780 or £800 hammer prices; or with the illustration charge £826 say £850 hammer price.

The Theory

If you want to be able to play tunes with the above figures, i.e. repeat the calculations for different situations, then the following theory may be of interest.

Buying at Auction

Let 'B' be the buying cost,

'b' be the buying hammer price,

'p' be the percentage buyer's premium divided by 100 (for example, if the buyer's premium is 15 per cent then 'p' equals 0.15)

'v' be the percentage rate of VAT divided by 100 (for example, if the VAT percentage is 17½, then 'v' equals 0.175).

Therefore, the buying cost ('B') equals the hammer price

('b') plus the buyer's premium plus the VAT on the buyer's premium:

$$B = b(1+p) + bpv = b[1+p(1+v)]$$

For example, if the hammer price was £500, the buyer's premium 15 per cent and VAT 17½ per cent, then the buying cost would be calculated as follows:

$$\begin{aligned} B &= £500[1+0.15(1+0.175)] \\ &= £500[1.15+0.026] \\ &= £500\times1.176 = £588 \end{aligned}$$

Selling at Auction

Let 'S' be the sales income,
's' be the selling hammer price,
'c' be the percentage sales commission plus insurance percentage divided by 100 (for example, if the sales commission is 10 per cent and the insurance percentage is 1½ per cent, then 'c' equals 10% + 1½% = 11½% divided by 100, i.e. 'c' equals 0.115) and 'v' be the percentage rate of VAT divided by 100, as above.

Therefore, the sales income ('S') equals the hammer price ('s') minus the sales commission and insurance minus the VAT on the sales commission and insurance:

$$S = s(1-c) - scv = s[1-c(1+v)]$$

For example, if the hammer price was £500, the commission rate 10 per cent and the insurance 1 per cent:

$$\begin{aligned} \text{The sales income } S &= £500[1-0.11(1+0.175)] \\ &= £500[1-0.11-0.019] \\ &= £500\times0.871 = £435.50 \end{aligned}$$

Breaking Even when Buying and Selling at Auction

Buying cost equals sales income, i.e. B = S:

i.e. b[1+p(1+v)] = s[1−c(1+v)], so that s = b[(1+p(1+v)] divided by 1−c(1+v)

Using the values already given above, the equation would read:

s = £500[1+0.15×(1.175) = £588 divided by 1−0.11(1.175)
= £588 divided by 0.871 = £675

i.e. with the assumptions made of 15 per cent buying premium and 10 per cent commission and 1 per cent insurance and the prevailing rate of VAT, if you pay a hammer price of £500 and then want to break even when selling at auction, the selling hammer price has to be £675. If there is an illustration charge of £40, which becomes £47 with VAT, this is dealt with by adding it to the buying cost. Thus the buying cost is now taken as £588 + £47 = £635, and if this is divided by 0.871 the selling hammer price for break even becomes £729.

Making a profit: If you wish to make a 20 per cent profit, then:

S = 1.2 times B, so that S = 1.2 times £588 divided by 0.871
= £810

with a £40 illustration cost, 1.2 times £635 divided by 0.871
= £875

The basic equation is:

s[1−c(1+v)] = Xb[1+p(1+v)] + X[i(1+v)].
where 'i' = illustration cost
'X' = (the percentage profit + 100) divided by 100
whence Xb[1+p(1+v)] = s[1−c(1+v)] − X [i(1+v)]
b = s[1−c(1+v)] − X[i(1+v)] all divided by
X[1+p(1+v)]

Buying at auction to make a profit against a firm selling price

If you have a client with whom you can agree a firm selling price for a picture that you are going to buy at auction, you need to work out the buying hammer price. If the client is willing to pay £600, and you want 20 per cent gross profit and are going to an auction house where the buyer's premium is 15 per cent:

$$Xb[1+p(1+v)] = £600$$

b = £600 divided by X[1+p(1+v)], i.e. by $1.2(1+ 0.15 \times 1.175) = 1.4115$

= £425

If you have bought elsewhere than at auction and wish to calculate the selling hammer price if you are planning to sell at auction, then your equations would be:

$$s[1-c(1+v)] = X B + X [i(1+v)]$$

whence: s = X B + X[i(1+v)] divided by 1−c(1+v)

If B = £500, X = 1.2, c = 0.11, v = 0.175 and i = £40, then:

s = $1.2\times500 + 1.2 \times 40 \times 1.175$ all divided by

$1-0.11 \times 1.175$

= 600 + 56 divided by 0.87075

= £753

Bibliography

Ayres, James, *The Artist's Craft* (Guild Publishing, 1985)

Benezit, E., *Dictionnaire critique et documentaire des peintres, sculpteurs, dessinateurs et gravure (1995)*

Curtis, Tony (ed. and Compiler), The Lyle Official Review – Paintings Price Guide 1994 (Lyle Publications, 1994)

Forrest, Tim and Kirkwood, John, *The Bonhams Directory 1993* (Kyle Cathie Ltd, 1992)

Hislop, Duncan, *Art Sales Index 1995/6* (Art Sales Index Ltd, 1983)

Johnson J. and Greutzner, A., *Dictionary of British Artists*, Vol. 4 (Antique Collectors' Club, 1990)

Lugit, Fritz, *Les Marques de collections de dessins et d'estampes* (Amsterdam, 1921, suppl., The Hague, 1956)

Mackenzie, Ian, *British Prints: Dictionary and Price Guide* (Antique Collectors' Club, 1987)

Mallalieu, H.L., *How to Buy Pictures: Practical Advice on All Aspects of the Art Market (Phaidon, 1984)*

Mallalieu, H.L., The Dictionary of British Watercolour Artists Up to 1920 (The Antique Collectors' Club, 1985)

Mayers International Auction Records (Published annually in France, obtainable from Hilmarton Manor Press)

Miller's Picture Price Guide 1996 (Miller, 1996)

Mills, John Fitzmaurice, *Collecting Now: Know Your Picture* (Ariel Books, 1984)

Mitchell, Peter, *An Introduction to Picture Collecting* (Arthur Barker, 1968)
Mould, Philip, *Sleepers – In Search of Lost Masters* (Fourth Estate, 1995)
Russell, Ronald, *Discovering Antique Prints* (Shire Publications, 1992)
Spalding, Francis, *Dictionary of British Art: 20th-century Painters and Sculptors*, vol. 6 (The Antique Collectors' Club, 1990)
Stout, George L., *The Care of Pictures – A History of Tools, Techniques and Materials* (Dover Publications, 1975)
Thieme-Becker, *Allgemeines Lexikon Der Bildenden Kunstler Des XX Jahrunderts*
Vollard, Ambroise, *The Recollections of a Picture Dealer* (Souvenirs d'un March and de tableaux translated from the French by Violet M. Macdonald; Dover Publications, 1978)
Waterhouse, Ellis, *Dictionary of British Art: 16th and 17th Century British Painters*, vol. 1 (The Antique Collectors' Club, 1988)
Waterhouse, Ellis, *Dictionary of British Art: British 18th. Century Painters*, vol. 2 (The Antique Collectors' Club, 1981)
Waters, Grant M., *Dictionary of British Artists Working 1900–1950* (Eastbourne Fine Art, 1975)
Who's Who in Art, 26th edition (The Art Trade Press Ltd, 1994)
Wood, Christopher, *Dictionary of British Art: The Dictionary of British Painters*, vol. 1. (The Antique Collectors' Club, 1995)
Wright, Christopher, *The Art of the Forger* (Gordon Fraser, 1984)

Index

Index

Index

Index